Mohammed Zahid completed his PhD in Middle Eastern Political Economy and Politics at the University of Leeds. He has published widely in international journals and consulted for a number of agencies and think tanks on a variety of Middle Eastern issues, in particular relating to political economy, internal Arab politics and security in North Africa and the Persian Gulf.

THE MUSLIM BROTHERHOOD

AND EGYPT'S SUCCESSION CRISIS

The Politics of Liberalisation and Reform in the Middle East

MOHAMMED ZAHID

I.B. TAURIS

LONDON · NEW YORK

Revised paperback edition published and reprinted in 2012 by I.B.Tauris & Co Ltd
6 Salem Road, London W2 4BU
175 Fifth Avenue, New York NY 10010
www.ibtauris.com

Distributed in the United States and Canada
Exclusively by Palgrave Macmillan
175 Fifth Avenue, New York NY 10010

ISBN: 978 1 78076 217 3

A full CIP record for this book is available from the British Library
A full CIP record for this book is available from the Library of Congress

Library of Congress catalog card: available

Printed and bound by CPI Group (UK) Ltd, Croydon, CR0 4YY
Camera-ready copy edited and supplied by the author

MIX
Paper from
responsible sources
FSC
www.fsc.org   FSC® C013604

This work is dedicated to my late mother, may God give her a blissful resting place in her final abode

CONTENTS

TABLES

ABBREVIATIONS

ERSAP	Economic Reform and Structural Adjustment Programme
GCC	Gulf Cooperation Council
GDP	Gross Domestic Product
IFIs	International Financial Institutions
IMF	International Monetary Fund
JDP	Party of Justice and Development
IAF	Islamic Action Front
LFSS	Labour Force Sample Survey
MB	Muslim Brotherhood
NDP	National Democratic Party
NGOs	Non-Governmental Organisations
OECD	Organisation for Economic Co-operation and Development
PAMSCAD	Programme of Action to Mitigate the Social Consequences of Adjustment
PLO	Palestinian Liberation Organisation
SDR	Special Drawing Rights
SFD	Social Fund for Development
SOEs	State Owned Enterprises
WB	World Bank
YMMA	Young Men's Muslim Association

ACKNOWLEDGEMENTS

I would like to begin by expressing my thanks to God for giving me the ability to start and finish this study. I would like to express gratitude to my family for helping me throughout my writing especially my mother and father.

My appreciation goes to many people. Professor Ray Bush has been a great help in providing useful and insightful comments on my work and for assisting me in my field work when I was located in Egypt for 6 months. I made a number of friends in Egypt which helped in the progress of my work. Dr Hassanien Kish, situated at the Center for Criminological and Sociological Research in Cairo was of great help in providing names of contacts and his personal insight into Egyptian life was of great value and benefit. Also, I would like to thank Dr Maha Abdel Rahman, located at the American University in Cairo, for providing advice and guidance during my stay in Egypt, which was much appreciated.

A number of friends made my stay in Egypt pleasant, which I had the fortune of coming to know. My friend Said al Banna, who I had the privilege of knowing in the UK, was of great help to me throughout my stay in Egypt. Also, friends such as Hassan and Hisham made my time in Cairo enjoyable by showing me around and always making me feel welcome into their homes. A special thanks goes to all the friends I made from the Al Diwan Language center in Cairo. I would like to thank Islam, Waleed, Ahmed, Saeed and all the other teachers at the centre for being a great help to me. My fellow students at the centre became great friends to whom I would like to express much gratitude as without their companionship Medinat al Nasr would have been a lonely place. There is no room to mention you all but a big thanks to my room mates Farooq, Umar, Kamran, Aseem and to Momin and his family, all of whom provided companionship in what became our infamous eating place, 'Sharkawy's'.

PREFACE

2011 has been a year of monumental change in Egypt, stemming from the uprising that removed President Hosni Mubarak and the ruling National Democratic Party (NDP) from government in February 2011. This historic event occurred after 18 days of continuous protests that united the country around the demand for an end to Mubarak's 30 years of oppressive rule and corruption.

But the aftermath of the 25th January revolution has been unsteady. As competing forces vie for a say in the course Egypt should take through its transition process, much debate has hinged on the fraught and fundamental question of whether Egypt should maintain its officially secular character, cultivated since the 1952 revolution, or move towards a more religious form of government. The rise of Islamist parties and their entry into the political system, through the new spaces that have opened up in post-Mubarak Egypt, has thrust this issue onto centre stage and fuelled secular and liberal fears of a takeover from the Islamists that would leave them marginalised.

The Muslim Brotherhood (MB), the leading Islamist group, endured decades of oppression under the Mubarak regime and attempts to create a political party were rejected by the NDP-dominated Political Parties Committee, confining them to the sidelines of mainstream politics. They are now able to operate openly and have taken full advantage of this new-found freedom by establishing a political party, *Hizb al Hurriya wa al Adala* or the Freedom and Justice Party (FJP), to represent the movement's political ambitions. The FJP's impressive showing in parliamentary elections that began in late 2011 – and were the first since Mubarak's fall – showcased their superior organisational capacities and secured them just under half of the vote to make them the largest bloc in the new parliament.

Meanwhile, the ultra-conservative Salafists have stirred from years of political slumber and quietism to become a significant force, with their newly-formed *Hizb al Nour* (Party of Light) that came in second, after the MB, in parliamentary elections to gain nearly a quarter of all seats. This emergence raises the spectre of alliance between these two leading Islamist groups, one that would secure a majority in parliament and dwarf secular and liberal parties.

The secular opposition is hampered by years of disorganisation, internal battles for leadership and a lack of ideological coherence. They had blamed the Mubarak regime for their declining position, and internal division has resulted in over 30 secular political parties competing in the parliamentary elections, which worked in the favour of Islamists, in particular the MB. Far more organised, robust and coherent, they have strengthened their support base across Egypt and leapt ahead in the polls.

However, at the time of writing, it is still the Egyptian military, headed by Mubarak's former Defence Minister Field Marshall Hussein Tantawi, who are running the show in Egypt. Hardly a new arrival on the political scene, the army, through the Supreme Council of the Armed Forces (SCAF), has taken on the task of steering Egypt through its transition process.

The now well-worn slogan *'al gaysh wa al shaab iyd wahda!'* ('the army and the people are one hand!') was originally chanted in Tahrir Square and pointed to an initial swell of support for the military, perceived by many as an institution of the revolution that had sided with the people during the 18 days of uprising. They had helped in the removal of Mubarak, and then put him, his sons and other prominent regime figures on trial.

However, discontent with SCAF's handling of the volatile situation in Egypt has grown. It has failed to meet many of the revolution's demands, in particular a quick transfer of power to a civilian government, leading to accusations that it has hijacked the revolution for its own interests. A series of violent crackdowns on protests, such as the Maspero massacre of mainly Coptic protestors in October 2011, the mistreatment of detainees, most controversially subjecting women to so-called 'virginity tests', the use of military trials to target civilians and a growing list of other abuses have all tarnished the image of the army in the eyes of the public. It has much to do to repair its reputation and build new bridges with the Egyptian people.

The relationship between the military and the MB, as the largest Islamist party, is set to be a crucial element of the path Egypt takes, and is subject to much debate and speculation. The military has been accused of making backdoor deals that allow the Islamist bloc to participate in the political system without obstructions, in return for protecting their interests. Meanwhile, when a new round of bloody protests in November 2011, triggered by the now infamous Silmi document in which the military sought to write their privileged position into the constitution, was met by a brutal and heavy-handed response from the army, the MB refused to join the demonstrations and faced allegations of betraying the revolution for their own pragmatic political interests – namely to ensure that the elections due to start the following week, that they were sure to do well in, went ahead at all costs.

Post-Mubarak Egypt is marred by uncertainties and the path forward littered with obstacles, but the MB are positioning themselves to dominate the political scene for years to come. The complex relationships between the diverse set of political actors that have emerged in this new environment, all competing for a share in a new Egypt, continues to unfold and shape an unpredictable transition process.

In order to understand the Egyptian revolution, it is important to look into the political and economic circumstances which caused the explosion into mass mobilisation and political action against the Mubarak regime at the start of 2011. Similarly, it is by looking into the Mubarak period that one will be able to understand the new set up which is emerging. The weak secular forces had been increasingly undermined by the state, but these groups themselves have played a role in their marginalisation throughout politics and society. This stands in stark contrast to the Islamist movements, who were able to expand and grow on a grass roots level under Mubarak, so as to emerge in 2011 with an extensive support base and a significant advantage over defunct secular opposition.

Mohammed Zahid
Cairo, December 2011

1

FRAMING ECONOMIC AND POLITICAL REFORM IN THE MIDDLE EAST

A causal relationship has been hypothesised between economic and political liberalisation, with the former viewed as a key driver in the process of political change (Friedman, 1962; Hayek, 1960). Economic liberalisation is believed to roll back the state, creating a political space in which civil society can develop. As civil-society groups proliferate, the argument runs, individuals become more assertive in demanding their political rights; and once these demands reach a certain level, authoritarian leaders are forced to make meaningful political changes, or risk being swept away (Cook, 2005). The policy implication of this connective relationship between economic and political liberalisation is simple: encourage economic liberalisation to promote the growth of civil society. The relationship has been central to the work of International Financial Institutions (IFIs) and aid agencies in the Middle East. However, establishing a link between economic and political liberalisation in the region has been problematic, because of two main factors. First, the level and extent of economic liberalisation has not been consistent – indeed, in most cases it has been restrictive and minimal. Second, regional crises such as the Arab-Israeli conflict, and border clashes such as between Saudi Arabia and Yemen or Iran and Iraq, have been continuously used by power elites to keep in place autocratic mechanisms and institutions. These two factors have made it problematic to examine the link between economic and political liberalisation in the region.

This book therefore does not aim to address the relationship, if any, between economic and political liberalisation in the Middle East, but it does seek to examine the process of economic and political change in Egypt, with particular reference to the period 1991–2009. I focus especially on the role of the Muslim Brotherhood (MB), and its role in the process of political change, by examining the changes it has itself undergone in its shape and character, which allowed it to become a key political actor in Egypt. I also look at the way in which the Egyptian state sought to manage and usher forward the politics of succession, by considering the actors and forces driving the succession process in Egypt.

In considering these issues, four important questions emerge. To what extent was there a process of economic and political reform in Egypt? To what extent did this process of change allow for the emergence of a functioning civil society? To what extent did this allow political actors such as the MB to challenge state power? Finally, to what extent was the role of the MB symptomatic of challenges to the legitimacy of the existing state dispensation? To address these questions, this book will first examine the process of economic and political reform in the wider Middle East; this is located in the context of regional and global developments such as US foreign policy post-9/11 and the subsequent 'War on Terror'.

The case of Egypt and the MB is detailed in Chapters 3–8, where the economic and political changes in Egypt are set out. In particular they provide an understanding of the process of political change by examining the details of the MB's transformation from a religious movement into a central political actor in

Egyptian politics. I examine how it emerged as a strong political force and how internal reforms of its organisation contributed to its increasing strength in Egyptian political life. I also situate these internal political and organisational transformations within the MB alongside shifts in the spiritual and ideological discourse that the MB promotes. By understanding these shifts, the process of change in the MB's shape and character and how it came to relate to the Egyptian state can be more readily understood. This will allow an understanding of how the MB became a key agent in Egyptian politics and how it was able to challenge the authority and possibly the hegemony of the Egyptian government. The importance of the MB in Egyptian politics and the increased interest in its role is related to the post-9/11 debate concerning democratisation in the Middle East, and the role of US foreign policy viewed as promoting democracy in the region. In this process of democratisation Egypt came to be viewed as a key actor in spearheading the process of political change, due to its close relationship with the US and its key regional role in the Middle East. Meanwhile, the MB was the single largest political force in Egypt, and post 1991 it became the main competitor with state power, which dramatically raised its profile. As a result the MB became central to the process of economic and political change in Egypt.

After a detailed examination of the MB I will explore the politics of succession in Egypt, which rose to the surface of Egyptian politics in recent years – as a result of the increasing power of Gamal Mubarak and his associates, whose rise in the political hierarchy raised many questions pertaining to the future direction of economic and political change in Egypt. It is therefore important to explore the discourse of political succession, taking into consideration the grooming process, the actors involved, and the forces driving political succession in the country. It is also important to examine the role of key political actors such as the MB and the military to determine the extent of their influence and impact on the political-succession process. This discussion will provide a basis for exploring the future process of economic and political change in Egypt, in particular the level of continuity and discontinuity in the process of economic and political change.

2

SHIFTING SANDS:
THE MIDDLE EAST BETWEEN
AUTHORITARIANISM AND
DEMOCRATISATION

This chapter will explore the process of economic and political change in the Middle East, considering the impact of processes of political change on state powers and structures. In doing this it is important to explore the following questions. To what extent has there been a process of economic and political reform in the Middle East? To what extent has this process allowed for the emergence of a functioning civil society? To what extent has this allowed political actors such as Islamist parties to challenge state power? Finally, to what extent is the role of the Islamist parties symptomatic of challenges to the legitimacy of the existing state dispensation? Also, it is important to examine US foreign policy post-9/11, to determine the extent to which it has promoted democracy in the Middle East.

Economic and political reform in the Middle East
The Middle East undertook economic reform in the 1980s and 1990s, with the 'Washington Consensus' laying down the reform programme (Williams, 1990; 1996; 1997). The key targets of the

consensus included the introduction of government budgetary balances, low inflation and market-determined prices, and the liberalisation of economic sectors (Dhumale, 2000; Harik and Sullivan, 1992; Erian et al, 1996). To achieve these targets economic reform was shaped by two key processes. The first was the macroeconomic stabilisation of the economy through the use of tight fiscal and monetary policies. The second was the structural adjustment of the economy, which involved a number of policies such as the removal of price controls, privatisation, the free floating of the currency and the liberalisation of key economic sectors (Easterly, 2001; Killick, 1995; Bird, 1995). However, the Arab states were somewhat inconsistent in carrying out economic reforms: they showed commitment to the process of macroeconomic stabilisation, but were less dedicated to structural adjustment, preferring a gradual approach in contrast to the 'shock approach' favoured by the IFIs. Two main reasons can be presented for this: First, a number of strikes and protests in the 1980s and 1990s, in response to economic policies such as the removal of price controls and privatisation, raised concerns among the power elites, and led them to pursue a more cautious method of structural adjustment (Sadiki, 2000; Burke, 1987). For example, in August 1983 the Moroccan government reduced consumer subsidies by 20 per cent, triggering urban unrest in the north and elsewhere. In Jordan, the abrupt way in which Jordanian government tried to raise fuel prices in 1989 incited riots in the southern city of Ma'an, resulting in the death of eleven people (Ryan, 1998). Similar protests and strikes took place in Tunis in 1984 and Khartoum in 1982 and 1985 (Bayet, 2003). The second reason is that powerful vested interests in society blocked economic reform, either directly or by ensuring the passage of specific reforms that led to capital accumulation.

As a consequence, the results were inconsistent: regimes embraced some economic reforms relating to macroeconomic stabilisation, yet postponed or evaded more complex measures relating to structural adjustment, such as privatisation, reform of regulatory rules and the development of the rule of law (Richards, 2001). For example, the Egyptian experience of economic reform in the 1990s is indicative of powerful vested interests blocking parts of economic reform which threatened their economic status. Members of the military-bureaucracy complex created by Nasser did not react favourably to market policies such as privatisation and the liberation of economic sectors (e.g. insurance and banking), due to the inevitable harming of their economic interests. As a result, the Nasser era saw the early formation of a close relationship between government officials, the military and the business class, and this led to a number of economic policies perceived as running counter to their status and interests being effectively blocked (Hirst, 1999).

As a result of these two factors (political risk and the role of vested interests), power elites embraced economic reforms relating to macroeconomic stabilisation, but often abandoned or evaded structural adjustments such as marketisation, privatisation, and reform of institutions and regulatory practices (Richards, 2001). Thus, Arab states walked a fine line between meeting economic reforms demanded by the IFIs and internal demands (i.e. from the public and vested interests). In particular, these states worked hard to minimise the socio-economic fallout by pursuing an inconsistent approach to economic reform. Despite this endeavour, the socio-economic changes in the region in the 1990s were worrying.

Socio-economic changes

The neo-liberal economic reforms of this period provoked a number of socio-economic changes. The market reforms made consumer commodities vastly more available, improving the living conditions of the upper socio-economic strata while also increasing income disparities and causing critical changes in labour markets. For example, there was a rapid increase in the size of informal and marginalised groups, such as the unemployed, casual workers and street-subsistence labourers (UNHDP, 2002; *The Economist*, 2002). The level of unemployment was worrying, and it continued to increase in the 1990s (Richards, 2001). The average unemployment rate for the six largest non-oil or diversified economies in the region (Syria, Algeria, Egypt, Iran, Morocco and Tunisia) rose from 12.7 per cent in 1990 to 15 per cent in 2000 (Gardner, 2003). In the 1990s more than one-third of Morocco's youth were unemployed, while in Syria youth unemployment was 73 per cent (Heydeman, 2004). Women in the Middle East were unemployed at twice the rate of men. Vast segments of the workforce were employed in the informal sector, with no access to the benefits of formal employment (Heydeman, 2003). A 2002 World Bank (WB) study of 16 countries in the Middle East and North Africa, representing some 60 per cent of the entire region's population, showed that up to 47 million new jobs would need to be created between 2002 and 2012 merely to keep pace with new entrants into the labour market (Keller and Nabli, 2002). An additional 6.5 million jobs would be needed to reduce the unemployment rate to just below 10 per cent. This indicated the challenge of unemployment in the Middle East; the levels can be seen from Table 2.1 below.

Table 2.1 Unemployment rates in the Middle East

Country	Rate (%)	Remarks
Algeria	30	Data from 1999.
Egypt	12	Data from 2000 (some estimates show 20%)
Iran	20–25	Data from 2001
Jordan	15	Official rate
Lebanon	18	Data from 1998
Libya	29	Data from 2000
Morocco	15–22	Data from 2000
Saudi Arabia	14–18	Higher among graduates
Syria	12–15	Data from 1999
Tunisia	16	Data from 1999
Yemen	35	Data from 1999

Sources: for Saudi Arabia, US Embassy, Riyadh, and *The New York Times*, 26 August 2001; for Iran, *Le Monde Diplomatique*, 5 June 2001; for all others, MEDEA Institute and CIA *World Fact Book*, 2001.

In the 1990s the socio-economic problems in the region were exacerbated by the economic withdrawal of the state. Many much needed social provisions were ended or cut, and low-income groups largely had to rely on themselves to survive. For instance, in Egypt state subsidies for basic foodstuffs such as rice, sugar and cooking oil were removed, and those for items such as fuel, power and transportation were reduced. Meanwhile, the reform of the public sector and the process of privatisation continued, with excessive social costs. Significantly, rent control was reconsidered through a new land law in 1992 which ended tenant farmers' control over land. In the early 1990s a number of international aid agencies, such as the US Agency for International Development (USAID), which has extensive operations in Cairo, was raising alert levels over the heightened socio-economic crisis in Egypt, with an increase in unemployment and poverty, made worse by the population drift from rural to urban areas (USAID, 1993; Westley, 1998; Amin, 1998). Similar socio-economic changes took place in Jordan, exacerbated by events such as the Gulf War in 1991, which deepened the country's crisis (Majdalani, 1999). In Iran, the government moved between statism and free-market policies in the 1990s. The direction and pace of economic liberalisation was slow, due to the political and economic struggle between rival political and economic factions, with each aiming to preserve their interests and resources (Bayat, 2000). In the midst of this struggle, the real losers were the Iranian public: the country experienced a socio-economic crisis in the 1990s, with conditions similar to those in Egypt and Jordan.

Overall, socio-economic changes in the Middle East were negative, notably the increasing levels of unemployment and poverty. In the 1990s these changes posed a danger to the survival, power and security of the Arab states, which, in reply to the growing socio-economic crisis, began to experiment with a process of political liberalisation – the strategic opening-up of political space in society to allow political participation, although limited in nature and scope. This was a drastic and significant change in the behaviour of the Arab states, which had previously been characterised by excessive authoritarianism; given this change, it is important to explore the process of political liberalisation in the Middle East during the 1990s, in particular to establish the extent to which the process allowed space for political actors to emerge and to contest the power of the state, its authoritarian mechanism and its structures.

The shift from authoritarianism to political liberalisation
During the late 1980s and the early 1990s, the careful blend and network of elite politics, patronage, controlled repression and patrimonialism in the Middle East were no longer viable or sustainable, as a result of the heightened socio-economic crisis being experienced by Arab states (Brumberg, 2002; Bromley, 1994; Niblock and Murphy, 1993). This heightened socio-economic crisis, which was exerting public pressure on the state, forced the political elite to change their attitudes and dispositions, leading to the reworking of embedded political rules and networks. This reworking of rules and networks in turn created the foundation for the process of political liberalisation in the region, allowing political actors of various ideological shades to enter the political system. For example, in Egypt parliamentary elections were held in 1990; Syria extended the number of seats in the legislature to include 60 independent members; the Gulf monarchs created consultative chambers; in 1989 Jordan held its first elections for a substantial period; and Yemen held elections in 1993 (Kechichian, 2004; Rumaihi, 1996; Nonneman, 2001; Bensahel and Byman, 2004; Ehteshami, 2003). A tide of political change was witnessed which brought much enthusiasm for reform and progress in the Middle East (Ibrahim, 1995; Sadiki, 1997). This excitement, however, did not last long, as it would become apparent soon after that the reworking of the rules and networks turned out not to weaken or eliminate the

mechanisms and structures which gave rise to authoritarianism in the region.

In Arab states governed by single, dominant parties, as in Syria, Tunisia and Egypt, the process of political liberalisation led to political manipulation rather than weakening state power and structures (Albrecht and Schlumberger, 2004). Political creativity and manipulation led to the break-up of existing political parties, resulting in turn in the creation of weak and insignificant entities which allowed the state to play each one off against the others; significantly, these new bodies also lacked popular support, adding to their ineffectiveness (Brumberg, 2002; Salame, 1994). The cunning political manipulation introduced by the Baathist regime in Syria perpetuated the personnel, networks and hidden relationships which, since the 1970s, had contributed to the Baathists' ingrained political secretiveness and to the maintenance of their control over Syrian politics. As a result of this clever political manoeuvring and manipulation by the Baathist party, its control over the liberalisation process led to the continuation of its influence and of its relationship with the important Sunni business and merchant class in Damascus and Aleppo (Brumberg, 2002). As for the monarchies, while they were not characterised by dominant ruling parties as in Egypt and Syria, the close links between the monarchy and opposition-party leaders nevertheless ensured what was often a remarkable level of consensus, and provided an opportunity for the monarchy to manipulate and co-opt political opposition through providing ministerial and institutional positions (Brumberg, 2002). The executive branch continued to dominate politics, with the influence and power of the executive emphasised in legislation and institutions. For example, Arab constitutions give immense power to the head of state, who has a key say in the appointment of ministers, in the allocation of budgets and in foreign policy, and also has the right to dissolve parliament. This is the case in numerous Arab countries, such as Egypt, Qatar and Saudi Arabia. In addition, the lack of clarity over the separation between the various branches of the political framework gives the upper hand to the heads of state, allowing political engineering and manipulation to prolong their stay in office. As a result of this arrangement, the early and mid-1990s was a period of conflict, deadlock and paralysis between the executive and the legislature on a range of issues such as electoral, party and press laws (Herb, 2002). The executive, which had mastered the art of political survival through cunning and manipulation, in fact introduced a new set of political reforms, effectively perpetuating and strengthening its own powers at a time of political liberalisation. This was often accomplished by creating an upper house whose appointed or indirectly elected members had the authority to block the legislation of the lower house, thus effectively defending and ensuring the supremacy of the executive. This was the case with constitutional reform in Morocco 1996, Algeria 1996, and Bahrain 2002.

Despite the fact that the process of political liberalisation did not weaken these states' powers and structures, the political opposition, including the secularists and Islamists, continued to accept and play by the new rules of the game set by the Arab states. A key reason for this acceptance by both factions was political expediency, as it allowed access to the channels of power and political exposure at the highest level. For secular and Islamic parties, entry into the political system was vital to their political ambitions, as it gave them insider status and so allowed them to contest state power and authority at the national level. In Algeria, Jordan and Yemen, political reforms of different varieties at different times made it possible for opposition parties (both secular and Islamic) to participate in multi-party cabinets. For example, in the mid-1990s the formation of a government in Morocco was led by the opposition. This would not have been possible if the opposition had failed to go along with the existing rules and with new ones introduced by the political elite. Thus the opposition entered state-managed power-sharing arrangements, whether in parliament or government, which has meant coordinating and co-operating not only with the political elite but also with each other, a breakthrough in the isolationist and dogmatic politics in the region (Brumberg, 2002). In 1997 Algeria introduced a modus operandi in which parliamentary seats were distributed among ideological foes such as the Islamists and liberals (Brumberg, 2002). Although the parliament had no real authority or power, operating as it did under the supervision of the military elite, it served the purpose of bringing together ideological rivals, and this played an important role in bringing a degree of stability and normality to Algeria after the civil war in the early 1990s. In certain Gulf states, such as Kuwait, the opposition – including the Islamists – have been operating as a body since the early 1990s, creating a very lively parliamentary institution, similar to that in Lebanon. On numerous occasions, the secularists and liberals have come together to challenge the state on a number of pertinent economic and political and economic issues, in particular foreign investment and privatisation. On a number of occasions, they have also tried to contest the complex set of formal and informal networks that allow the Kuwaiti royal family to prevent the political opposition from having a dominant role in parliament (Brumberg, 2002; Crystal, 1990). Kuwait's relatively open society gives secular and Islamist forces opportunities to express themselves in parliament and through a variety of newspapers and civil-society institutions. As a result political opponents are allowed to convey their messages to the Kuwaiti electorate, which would have been more difficult if they had refused to enter the political system and worked according to defined rules and parameters set by the Kuwaiti hierarchy.

As in Kuwait, secularists and Islamists found a niche for themselves inside political systems across the Middle East in the 1990s. However, the secular opposition lacked a strong social and grass-roots base, and thus a strong existence outside the system, which would have allowed it to exert bottom-up and top-down pressure on the state. In contrast, the Islamists used their existence outside the system (i.e. their social base and networks) to assist their agenda inside the political system, Egypt being a clear case of this strategy. Also, the work of Islamists was facilitated by the proliferation of civil-society organisations in the 1990s, which allowed Islamists to exert a greater degree of outside pressure on state power and its structures. The Arab state, which found itself unable to cope with the manifold social, economic and humanitarian challenges resulting from failed economic policies, allowed non-governmental or quasi-non-governmental groups to initiate a number of programmes in health, employment, training, the environment and education. Importantly, long-standing professional associations, representing lawyers, journalists, businessmen, academics, doctors and engineers, also became more active and politicised as they attempted to address the growing socio-economic crisis and to substitute for weak secular political parties. In particular this opening-up of space in civil society provided further room for Islamist parties and organisations to mobilise outside the system in order to contest and challenge state power, thus testing the liberalising credentials of Arab states by launching a challenge to state power both from inside the system and from outside, through civil society. They therefore provided a new, two-dimensional challenge to the Arab state, which it either had to respond to or face the prospect of having its powers severely checked – or, an even more worrying scenario, to face losing those powers as a new political environment emerged.

Civil society, Islamist politics and their challenge to the Arab state

In the light of its very close association with the democratic process, the Western construct of civil society has for some time been at the centre of discussion and debate in academic and policy-making circles in the West (Cavatorta, 2006). In Western academic and policy making discourse, it is believed that the existence of an independent space between the state and the individual is fundamental to a democratic political system, as the space allows groups and organisations to emerge and to represent diverse interests in society. These groups and organisations provide a means of not only representing diverse interests but also allowing society to develop and strengthen networks, ties and relationships through meetings, gatherings, activity and mobilisation (Gellner, 1994). These positive outcomes and implications that an active civil society has in Western democratic countries have been transferred to authoritarian states. The ability of independent social groups and organisations to create an independent space for action, away from the overbearing and obtrusive state, is viewed as vital in undermining and weakening the authoritarianism that exists in such states (Norton, 1994–95). The existing academic literature on democratic transitions focuses on the role of civil society in the movement away from authoritarianism and towards democratic political systems, in particular investigating transitions in Latin America, Africa and post-communist Eastern Europe. This literature supports the hypothesis linking civil society to democratisation by showing that countries with a growing and robust civil society were either democratic or in the process of becoming democratic. While countries with a weak and passive civil society had authoritarian networks and mechanisms so embedded that there was no prospect of them being shaken or weakened (Cavatorta, 2006). With regard to the Middle East, early academic studies, strongly influenced by Orientalist scholarship, painted a negative picture of political activity in the region, with culture, religion and Muslim mind-sets blamed for the stagnant political climate there (Mardin, 1995). However, Norton's (1995–96) seminal and extensive academic study of civil society in the region contradicted much of this previous scholarship, which had painted a negative picture of the emergence and development of civil society in the region. His study demonstrated that civil activism in the Middle East had in fact been largely ignored in the academic world, which raised question-marks over previous scholarship on civil society in the region. According to a number of academics, such as Bayet and

Nonneman, the study by Norton was a landmark investigation into society in the region, refuting previous misconceptions about the absence of civil society, while presenting the breadth and depth of the subject across the region (Bayet, 2000; Nonneman, 2001). While Norton's study was a major breakthrough, and quickly became the accepted analysis, it still left open serious questions surrounding the problem of Middle Eastern authoritarianism. This was because it could no longer be maintained that the lack of democracy in the Middle East was due to the absence of civil society – Norton had demonstrated that civil society did indeed exist in the region.

Given the findings of Norton, it could not now be argued that a civil society did not exist in the region, and as a result a number of academics began to present new arguments to explain the absence of democracy there, such as the existence of Islamist organisations. The latter are perceived by some Western observers, such as Sami Zubaida and Amy Hawthorne, as strengthening authoritarianism rather than creating an environment conducive to democratic change (Cavatorta, 2006). For example, many secularist writers in the West and the Middle East have sought to remove Islam from any definition of civil society, reasoning that religion-centred societies are incompatible with liberal democracy and more conducive to patriarchies, with power concentrated in the hands of an individual or a small elite (Zubaida, 2001; Cavatorta, 2006).

At the foreign-policy level, a number of academics and policy institutes have warned the US about the role of Islamist actors in Arab civil society: they are seen as unfavourable towards democracy, even though they may deploy its rhetoric (Cavatorta, 2006; Hawthorne, 2004). Although Hawthorne emphasises the positive role religion has played in democratic transitions in Latin America and Eastern Europe, she is not as receptive towards Islamist organisations. Like Berman, she highlights the case of Egypt, where Islamists have a stronghold in civil society and provide a number of services, leading secularists and civil-society sceptics to argue that civil society is not necessarily a force for good, depending as it does on those involved and engaged in it (Hawthorne, 2004; Berman, 2003)

This explanation, that authoritarianism in the Middle East remains embedded and robust because civil society is dominated by Islamists, which prevents it from triggering a real process of democratic political change, faces a number of shortcomings (Cavatorta, 2006; Brumberg, 2002). Cavatorta has mentioned a number of key findings which challenge this narrative of Islamists being an obstacle to the reform process. First of all, Cavatorta claims, the labelling of all Islamists as undemocratic does not reflect reality. Certain Islamists strongly emphasise their democratic beliefs and political behaviour, such as the Tunisian Nahda Party or the Algerian Movement for Society and Peace. Even the Egyptian Muslim Brotherhood, which has been highly criticised by Western policy makers, has been vocal about its commitment to democratic ideals and principles, demonstrated through its participation in state institutions since the 1980s. Also, importantly, Islamists are not homogenous, as they differ from one another in ideology, approach, structure, organisation, networks, relationships, leadership styles and mobilisation strategies (Cavatorta, 2006). Therefore to assume that they are all the basically the same because of shared Islamic beliefs is incorrect and misleading, and not helpful to the political reform-process in the region (Norton, 1995; Schwedler, 1998; 1998–99). According to Cavatorta, the second shortcoming is the empirical focus on groups which resort to violence to achieve their aims and objectives. This focus fails to take into consideration those Islamists who are non-violent, which constitute the majority of Islamists and who represent large sectors of society that struggle to have a voice and be represented, such as women from a deprived upbringing, and young people, who together constitute a large percentage of the population in the Middle East (Cavatorta, 2006). Again according to Cavatorta, the third shortcoming, is that to argue that democracy is absent in the region because of the existence of Islamists in civil society underestimates the nature of the Arab states, which are highly repressive and rely heavily on a 'coercive apparatus', to stay in power (see Posusney, 2004). As a result of these shortcomings highlighted by Cavatorta, it seems misguided to label civil society in the Arab world as authoritarian simply because of the role of Islamists; the latter operate in a certain political reality, where competing views and ideas are present – from alternative sources, such as liberals and communists – and they have to come to terms and deal with this reality to survive and work inside the political system. It becomes imperative to examine Islamist oppositions and their contribution to the process of political reform, to challenge misconceptions concerning their presumed 'totalitarian' social and political activism. This can be explored by examining three Islamist parties, which exist inside and outside the system in Jordan, Morocco and Bahrain.

The Jordanian Muslim Brotherhood – the Islamic Action Front

The Jordanian MB has long been integrated into the political mainstream, because it accepts the legitimacy of the Hashemite monarchy. It has been tacitly recognised first as a charitable and later as a quasi-political organisation, which has openly fielded candidates in parliamentary elections, albeit under a different name – the Islamic Action Front (IAF). The relationship between the MB and the monarchy has been beneficial for the former over the years, allowing it to expand its influence in Jordan. Jordanian monarchs have found the MB more useful politically as an ally than as an opponent, since it secured Islamist support in countering Arab nationalism during the 1960s and secular Palestinian nationalism in the 1970s (Tamimi, 1999). Jordanian Islamists have been most effective in gaining control of the country's educational system. After the Brotherhood sided with King Hussein during the Black September crisis of 1970, in which the Palestinian Liberation Organisation openly clashed with the Jordanian armed

forces, King Hussein granted the MB control over the Education
Ministry. Through its extensive charitable networks, the MB has
also established a number of Sunni Muslim schools (*madhaheb*), in
addition to institutions of higher education. The MB's educational,
social, and health services have grown so extensive over the years
that some experts believe that the MB budget for services rivals that
of the Jordanian government. In 1992, the MB's political wing,
the IAF, was legally recognised as a political party in Jordan under
a new political party law, which allowed the MB to be represented
at the national level. Three years before that, Jordanian Islamists
running as independents gained almost 40 per cent of the seats
in parliament. The government responded by altering the electoral law, changing the system from a multiple/transferable vote
system in which voters could cast as many ballots as there were
seats in their constituency, to a one-person, one-vote system which
led most voters to choose candidates from their extended families
or tribes over ideological parties such as the IAF (Clark, 2004).
Those who did vote for the IAF hailed predominately from urban
areas dominated by middle-class Jordanians of Palestinian origin.
Government-IAF relations deteriorated after the 1994 peace agreement with Israel, which resulted in the government constraining
IAF political activity to mosques and professional syndicates. In
response the IAF boycotted the 1997 elections. The parliamentary
elections held on 17 June 2003 gave 62 seats in the 110-member
lower house to conservative, independent and tribal allies of King
Abdullah. However, the IAF won 22 per cent of the vote, thereby
gaining 18 seats in the lower house, plus six sympathisers. When
asked about the IAF's prospects in future elections, one member
reportedly remarked that:

> I am not optimistic that we can win a majority now,
> because the laws have still not been changed … But we are
> not trying to take everything away. We just want to take
> part in a fair process. (*New York Times*, May 2006)

During 2007, the IAF faced the prospect of two elections, municipal and national. The IAF hoped both these would be free and fair and would allow the IAF to project its power and make further gains in Jordan. The IAF presented 25 candidates for the municipal elections, but on the eve of polling withdrew its candidates, accusing the authorities of manipulating votes cast by military personnel, who were taking part in municipal elections for the first time. This manipulation at the municipal level did not bode well for the national elections, in which, four months later (on 20 November 2007), the IAF fielded 22 candidates for the Jordanian national elections. Of the 22 candidates, only six successfully won parliamentary seats, marking the lowest showing of the Islamist party since the resumption of parliamentary life in Jordan in 1989. The IAF attributed its loss to the Jordanian government overlooking illegal practices such as vote-buying, the transfer of large numbers of votes, and inserting equally large numbers of voting cards into ballot boxes.

Despite the political manipulation of successive Jordanian elections to weaken the political representation of the Islamist party, the IAF continues to work in the political system to have a voice at the national level. This has allowed it to speak on economic issues such as corruption, privatisation and poverty, but also political issues such as political freedom and transparency, and even sensitive matters such as the peace agreement with Israel. The IAF is firmly embedded in Jordan through the MB, and is likely to apply more pressure to the Jordanian state in future through the social networks it has at its disposal. However, the state is continuing to make life difficult for the movement, recently banning independent religious edicts given without state approval, constraining the activity of the MB, and at the same time weakening the IAF by stripping four IAF MPs of their political immunity and imprisoning them. It is likely that this awkward relationship between the IAF and the Jordanian state will continue, but there is no doubt that the Jordanian Islamists have contributed new and different ideas to the discourse on economic and political reform in Jordan, and are likely to continue to do so, in particular as their grassroots support and strength grow.

The Moroccan MB – the Party of Justice and Development (JDP)

The JDP is one of a number of Islamic organisations in Morocco, but it is the only one which is involved in the political system, having adopted a path of involvement rather than disengagement (Christian Science Monitor, November 2005). The leadership of the JDP wished to strike a balance between continuing its opposition to government corruption and nepotism and preparing the ground for participation in future government coalitions. Reportedly, the JDP covets the influential Social Affairs and Education ministerial portfolios, where it could pursue its agenda of promoting Islamic morals and ethics in society. The JDP's aggressive campaigning among lower- and middle-class Moroccans has made the group more popular than many of Morocco's older and more established parties (Hamzawy et al. 2006). However, despite a growing support base, the JDP has decided to remain limited in its demands to consolidate its position, in the hope of launching a stronger challenge to the government in the future (Cavatorta, 2006). For example, the JDP remains allied with the monarchy, even on issues that would appear to contravene Islamic law, such as their acceptance of King Muhammad's 2004 ground-breaking revision of the family code (*mudawana*), which, among other things, raised the legal age of marriage for women from 15 to 18 and allowed women, with a judge's approval, to divorce their husbands. The JDP argued that because the revision of the family code was democratically enacted, its members should accept it, since the party was committed to both democratic and Islamic principles (Hamzawy et al, 2006). Despite this warming to the monarchy, for reasons of political opportunism and pragmatism, the JDP has done more than existing oppositional actors by campaigns to bring more transparency to Moroccan politics; for example, the party publishes the parliamentary attendance records of all MPs, in order to highlight the chronic absenteeism found in other parties. The JDP's leaders require its parliamentarians to attend all legislative sessions, and to be more productive than members of other parties. It is clear that the JDP has brought something different to Moroccan politics. The party's time in the system has been short, however, and it requires more time to develop as a political force, and then to contest the state effectively.

The Bahraini Shiites – the Al Wefaq National Islamic Society
Led by Sheikh Ali Salman, Al Wefaq is the largest Shiite bloc in Bahrain, with some 1,500 active members. It has based its appeal on the provision of social services and mosque outreach-programmes in both urban and rural areas. King Hamad's political reform process in 1999 provided a window of opportunity for Al Wefaq to enter the political system. The King's reform process, which he was not forced into, arguably stemmed from a generational change fuelled by his realisation that a new post-traditional Persian Gulf is emerging, in which tribal affiliations may no longer suffice to legitimise a ruling tribe (Wright, 2006). Therefore, since the start of his reign, King Hamad has promoted reforms characterised as liberalising, thus maintaining control of the pace and direction of political reform, and avoiding loss of political and economic privileges on the part of the elite. On the other hand, Bahrain's Shiite population, led by Al Wefaq, have sought a more fundamental political reorientation which, if allowed, would undermine King Hamad's current centralised power-base. The 2002 parliamentary elections provided a chance for Al Wefaq to enter the political system, but instead it boycotted those elections. That year there was widespread protest and political opposition led by Al Wefaq to the legislative rights granted to the 40 royally appointed members who formed the upper house of parliament and constituted a

distinctly unrepresentative majority loyal to the King (*Middle East International*, February 2004).

However, despite its boycott, Al Wefaq challenged legislation passed by the old parliament, specifically arguing for the need to revoke the Law of Associations, the Counter-Terrorism Law and the Law of Assembly. According to Bahraini and international human-rights groups, these laws have been misused to rein in civil liberties and dissent in Bahrain (*Gulf Daily News*, October 2006). In addition to this it called for constitutional reforms, which would weaken the monopolisation of power by the Bahraini state. These demands and challenges by Al Wefaq exerted a good deal of pressure on the state, in particular because of Al Wefaq's strong social support-base in Bahrain.

In its challenge to the Bahraini state Al Wefaq was willing to cross ideological barriers and to hold meetings with the secular opposition in Bahrain to achieve common goals. This led it to become a key political movement in Bahrain, and put it in a prime position to make major inroads in the 2006 parliamentary elections – in which it put forward 19 candidates for the 40 seat parliament, winning 18. Immediately after this victory Al Wefaq outlined its political aims, such as redrawing the constituency boundaries, providing more independence for local councils, and campaigning for constitutional reforms (*Gulf Daily News*, November 2006). In addition it vowed to strengthen its relations with opposition actors to give the opposition as a whole the ability to challenge the Bahraini state in the future.

Common Trends

The three case studies examined above highlight the key role Islamist parties have come to play both inside and outside the system in Jordanian, Moroccan and Bahraini politics. This is also this trend in other Arab states, such as Lebanon, the Palestinian Territories, Algeria, Kuwait, Yemen and Egypt. Thus, excluding non-violent Islamists from the political sphere only serves to weaken the chances for political transformation in the region. In fact, Arab secular liberals have come to realise this reality, and in the past few years have been gradually reaching out to Islamist parties and engaging them in reform campaigns. National secular-religious alliances for reform in the region are viewed as being instrumental in contesting authoritarian state power and its networks (Hamzawy, 2005). Islamists have seized the integration opportunity which has fallen to them, and positioned themselves strategically at the heart of growing opposition movements across the region. In Morocco, Lebanon and Egypt, there remain significant differences between liberals and Islamists, but the degree of convergence between the two groups over national priorities is growing systematically. The secular opposition has realised that political opposition platforms are far more effective with Islamist participation than without it, as they allow access to people whom secular parties cannot normally access or mobilise. It is likely that Islamist parties will continue to play a key role in the process of political reform, a role facilitated by the pressure they are able to apply to the state because of their dual existence – they have a presence both inside and outside the system. However, despite the positive contribution of Islamists to the process of change in the region, they face a number of obstacles which have hindered and will hinder their activities in the future, limiting and constraining them from effectively driving further the process of political reform. It is important to understand these obstacles and the impact they will have on the future reform process in the region.

Islamists and obstacles to change in the Middle East

Islamists have developed into key political actors, and are firmly entrenched in the political landscape of the Middle East. However, they face a number of obstacles in their quest to change the rules and networks of the political game. The first obstacle is the growing convergence and interaction between the state and business sectors.

This is a process by which individuals from the state apparatus, and (in the Gulf) from royal families, are active in economic and business ventures, and so step over into the private sector. This involvement has allowed the state to co-opt the business class, through the provision of economic resources and privileges, which in turn has strengthened the state's political arm, as the private sector has integrated itself into the state in return for opportunities to accumulate capital (Richards, 2001; Nonneman, 2001; Hinnebusch, 2001). This has resulted in the creation of a powerful bloc, a state-business nexus, which has resisted the economic and political changes sought by political actors such as Islamists, as such changes could endanger its economic and political interests.

A state-business nexus and relationships of such a nature were evident under Hafez Al Assad in Syria (Seale, 1990; Hinnebusch, 2001; Gambill, 2001; *Washington Post*, 28 October 2005). Breaking with Baathist socialist traditions, Assad gave greater latitude to the private sector, which was dominated, particularly in Damascus, by the Sunni urban economic and commercial elite. As a result of this limited economic opening (*infitah*), and with the growth of collusive state-business relations, large-scale Sunni entrepreneurs allied themselves with the regime in the 1980s, when Islamists challenged the state's power and its structures (*Al Ahram*, 6–12 April 2006). This nexus of the state and the Sunni commercial classes continues to exist in Syria, as Bashar Al Assad persists in pursuing pragmatic economic policies which benefit them. A comparable state-business nexus can be seen in Jordan and Egypt, where, as in Syria, it has constrained economic and political changes. To take the case of Jordan: since the inheritance of power by King Abdullah in 1999, the country has seen the overt introduction of the business class into national politics. The Jordanian state and its business class are more intertwined than ever before, resulting in the creation of a powerful bloc which has impeded the economic and political changes demanded by opposition such as the Islamists.

In Egypt under Mubarak, the ruling National Democratic Party (NDP), was full of individuals with business and commercial interests who blocked the reformist demands of the Islamists. This business class was further buttressed by the rise of Gamal Mubarak. Real estate tycoon Ahmed Bahgat, steel and iron industry chief Ahmed Ezz (who was also head of the People's Assembly's Planning and Budget Committee), former housing committee chief Mohammed Abul Enein, former head of the American Chamber of Commerce Mohammed Shafiq Gabr, the Sawiris family and business man and former parliamentarian Rami Lakah all came to be known for their privileged relations with the powers that be, and for their ability to influence decisions related to privatisation and the process of economic liberalisation (*Al Ahram*, 7–13 June 2001; Ghobashy, 2003). The Egyptian parliamentary elections in 2005 saw more candidates with business links than ever before, indicating the rise of big business in Egyptian politics and its role becoming more overt than ever before (*Al Jazeera*, 14 December 2005).

The second obstacle facing Islamists is the ever-powerful military, which has played its part in blocking economic and political reform. In countries such as Syria and Egypt the military leadership benefits from, and thus seeks to maintain, authoritarian political systems. The institutional power of Egypt's military establishment is reflected in the pattern of relations, following the 1952 revolution, between the presidency, its military-affiliated personnel, and the parliament (Abdalla, 2003). For example, these relations can be seen in the staff of the presidency, which has been composed almost exclusively of serving or retired military officers, with a significant role in the administration of the Egyptian state (Cook, 2004). They were routinely deployed throughout the various ministries and government agencies, to impress upon the vast Egyptian bureaucracy the priorities not only of the state but also of the military leadership. Furthermore, while issues relating to the allocation and procurement of arms, particularly from foreign suppliers, were legally subject to parliamentary review, this has never occurred (Cook, 2004).

Despite the wide-ranging powers of oversight which the People's Assembly was formally vested with, there was effectively no oversight of defence and security issues. Egypt's Defence Minister was formally required to make an annual presentation to the Assembly's standing committee on defence, national security and mobilization and to answer parliamentarians' questions. However, the presentation rarely occurred and when it did there was no thorough questions and probing, as the committee was dominated by NDP loyalists (Cook, 2004). The military was able to preserve its power over state institutions, and this allowed it to extend its reach into other areas, such as the economy. For example, the Egyptian government facilitated military expansion into the economic sector through the 'administration of national service projects', created in January 1979 (Zohny, 1987). In the 1990s, the economic power of the military increased, through its involvement in a number of development projects, such as canal and housing construction. The political and economic power thus accruing to the Egyptian military led to its blocking of the economic and political reform advocated by the political opposition – reform that could weaken its power by changing the existing rules and networks in Egypt. In particular, the military kept its eye on the Islamic movement, and was ever-willing to help the government in its battles against the Islamic movement in the 1980s and 1990s. The military, fully aware that the existing formal and informal rules and networks preserved its power, and that this made it unlikely that an inclusive Islamic movement such as the MB could seriously damage its interests. The military's concern was the prospect of outside pressure, which the MB could mobilise to antagonise the masses against the state and its institutions; this was a major worry for the military, and a reason to monitor the MB.

The third obstacle which Islamist parties have faced is the political elite, in particular its reluctance to relinquish political power. For example, Yemeni President Ali Abdullah Saleh, the second longest-serving leader in the Middle East after Colonel Muammer Gaddafi of Libya, announced in 2005 that he would not stand in the 2006 presidential elections, clearing the way for new blood to enter Yemeni politics (Phillips, 2006; 2005). However, this decision was reversed in 2006, with President Saleh announcing that he aimed to stand for another term in that year's presidential elections; and there was little doubt that Saleh would win these elections, given his monopoly over politics in Yemen (Philips, 2006). Importantly, what this indicated was the lack of any genuine desire on the part of the Yemeni political elite to relinquish power and to hand over the reins to fresh political blood. However, issues such as the growing socio-economic crisis and civil war in parts of the country could possibly be used by the Islamists as levers to further their political agenda.

It is thus clear that Islamist parties face a number of key obstacles in their agenda to rework the rules and networks of the political game in the region. However, the strategic positioning of Islamists at once inside and outside the system gives them the best opportunity and the most effective leverage to weaken and overcome these obstacles, in order to challenge state power and authoritarianism. However, to help further the process of economic and political change in the Middle East, there is a need for external actors to contribute to that process; and given the central role of the US in the region, it is important to examine US foreign policy there post-9/11.

The 'War on Terror' and US foreign policy towards the Middle East

In the 1990s, President Clinton supported the strategic liberalisation of political systems in the Middle East. Officials in his administration spoke of 'improved governance', 'political participation', 'pluralism' and 'greater openness' in the Middle East (Gause, 2005; Windsor, 2003; Regan, 2005). The US was trying 'to improve the climate for political liberalisation in the region', according to a 1995 statement by the then Assistant Secretary of State for Near Eastern Affairs, Robert H. Pelletreau. However, pro-democracy initiatives remained at the level of 'low policy', meaning they were neglected or undermined at the more influential diplomatic level when they conflicted with core 'high policy' interests such as regional security and the supply of oil. This was disclosed by the then Secretary of State, Madeleine Albright:

> We did nudge at times, supporting Kuwaiti leaders in their initiative to give women the vote and encouraging the creation of representative bodies in Bahrain and Jordan. But we did not make it a priority. Arab public opinion after all can be rather scary. (2003: 5)

Therefore, despite numerous pro-democracy programmes and lofty rhetoric, nowhere in the Arab world was the promotion of democracy a decisive force in US policy. At no time did an Arab regime's growing levels of authoritarianism directed towards the political opposition and civil society ever prompt the US administration to undertake any counter-measures. In contrast, President Clinton punished regimes in Latin America, Asia and Africa with sanctions in response to similar showings of excessive oppression and force towards the opposition and civil society. At no time in the 1990s was the promotion of democracy in the Arab world elevated to the level of other key US interests or, more crucially, integrated with them (Koh, 2001). However, post-9/11 changing international dynamics resulted in such promotion in the Middle East receiving more interest than ever before from the US administration. A key reason for this has been the link between authoritarianism and terrorism (Gause, 2005). The linkage is simple, following the line that authoritarianism leads to political exclusion and frustration, which leaves young men open to recruitment into terrorist organisations. By promoting democracy, it is argued that this sequence will be broken by empowering young men by giving them a greater say in how their state and society function and operate (Gause, 2005). To combat terrorism and to strengthen national security the US moved democracy promotion from a low- to a high-policy priority. President Bush made this clear in a series of keynote speeches. For instance, in developing a case for removing Saddam Hussein from power, Bush stated: 'The world has an interest in the spread of democratic values. A new regime in Iraq would serve as a dramatic and inspiring example of freedom for other nations in the region' (*New York Times*, 27 February 2003). In a speech at the University of South Carolina (9 May 2003), Bush outlined the US commitment to promoting democracy in the Middle East:

> We support the advance of freedom in the Middle East, because it is our founding principle ... the hateful ideology of terrorism is shaped by oppressive regimes ... free nations, in contrast, encourage creativity, tolerance, and enterprise ... over time, the expansion of liberty throughout the world is the best guarantee of security throughout the world.

President Bush once again referred to this commitment in a speech to the National Endowment for Democracy (6 November 2003), stating:

> Peoples of the Middle East share a high civilisation, a religion of personal responsibility and a need for freedom as deep as our own. It is not realism to suppose that one-fifth of humanity is unsuited to liberty, it is pessimism and condescension and we should have none of it.

This US commitment to the promotion of democracy in the Middle East was given further impetus when Bush, in a speech at the Royal Banquet House in London (19 November 2003), criticised previous US governments for failing to address the issue:

> Willing to make a bargain, to tolerate oppression for the sake of stability, long-standing ties often led us to overlook local elites. Yet this bargain did not bring stability or make us safe. It merely bought time, while problems festered and ideologies of violence took hold.

The presidential agenda was backed by senior US officials. Dick Cheney, the then Secretary of Defense, in a speech to the World Economic Forum (24 January 2004), stated:

> Our forward strategy for freedom commits us to support those who work and sacrifice for reform across the greater Middle East. We call upon our democratic friends and allies everywhere and in Europe in particular, to join us in this effort.

And Colin Powell, the Secretary of State, declared: 'Dictators and despots can build walls high enough to keep out armies, but not high enough to keep those winds from blowing in' (*Dawn News*, 12 November 2003). Michael Ledeen, a neo-conservative scholar close to President Bush, wrote: 'We should … be talking about using all our political, moral and military genius to support a vast democratic revolution to liberate all the people of the Middle East from tyranny' (*Wall Street Journal*, 4 September 2004).

In his Second Inaugural Address, on 20 January 2005, President Bush confirmed the notion that the 'forward strategy of freedom' – the promotion of democracy – and American security were closely interrelated: 'The survival of liberty in our land increasingly depends on the success of liberty in other lands' (*The Guardian*, 21 January 2005). Also, the National Security Strategy of 2006 put the spreading of democracy abroad at the centre of American security policy:

> In the world today, the fundamental character of regimes matters as much as the distribution of power among them. The goal of our statecraft is to help create a world of democratic, well-governed states that can meet the needs of their citizens and conduct themselves responsibly in the international system. This is the best way to provide enduring security for the American people.

Thus a revision in US foreign policy, directed towards the promotion of democracy in the Middle East, became apparent under the Bush administration. This kick-started a debate in the US foreign-policy community on the extent to which it should play a role in US policy towards the Middle East (Neep, 2004). The classical realists in that community, who are quick to dismiss the internal situation and realities of other countries as irrelevant to foreign-policy agendas and decision-making, were highly critical of President Bush's new policy in the Middle East (Speck, 2006). They argued that to promote democracy in the region would open a Pandora's box leading to destabilisation, and put at risk American national interests, such as energy security (i.e. access to oil and gas in the region) (Speck, 2006).

The fact that elections in Iraq, Egypt and the Palestinian Territories had seen the rise of Islamist parties reinforced the argument of the classical realists that autocratic regimes such as those in Egypt and Saudi Arabia might be bad, but opening up their political systems would allow hostile actors to come into play, which were much worse and not conducive to American economic and strategic interests (see *Washington Post*, 6 June 2005; *Guardian*, 9 December 2005; *Guardian*, 20 January 2006; BBC News, 26 January 2006). Thus, according to classical realists, a democratic transformation of the region bore such high risks that it was much more prudent to maintain the status quo, as the lesser evil (Guazzone, 1995). This classical-realist view was strengthened by opinion polls showing rising support for Islamic movements and a report released by the National Security Council on the 13 January 2004, which predicted that by 2020 a 'global caliphate' would have been established in the Middle East (CIA, 2004). Classical realists had always warned of a competitor and rival to US global interests; the emergence of a caliphate would cause serious problems for US interests in the Middle East. They therefore argued for keeping the existing systems and elite as they were, to block an Islamic movement from taking power and putting in place an alternative, Islamic model of government which could damage US interests.

Leftist critics, who had long been very critical of American foreign policy in the Middle East, charged that democracy promotion was a new cover for an old US policy, one that was still interest-driven. Thus, behind the liberal rhetoric lurked the old hypocrisy of American imperialism and the control of Middle Eastern economic resources. The Bush administration's reluctance to press Saudi Arabia, its close ally and third-largest oil supplier, towards democratic reform seemed to make it all too clear to leftist critics that the US government was far from giving up its double standards. Other critics challenged the diagnosis at the centre of the policy of promoting democracy (Speck, 2006); this issue arose after Islamist attacks on European soil. These attacks, especially the London bombings in July 2005, seemed to provide clear evidence that the breeding grounds for terrorism were not necessarily in the Middle East, but in Europe itself, with its large Muslim minorities that it had arguably failed to integrate. The revision of US policy has come under much scrutiny and criticism in the US itself; however, the gravest damage to the Bush administration's democratic agenda has been caused by the Iraq war.

As no weapons of mass destruction (WMD) were found in Iraq, making the country a beacon of democracy in the Middle East became a major motive and source of legitimacy for the war. This damaged US democracy promotion agenda in two ways. First, it made Iraq the test case in the region; but security failures in Iraq reinforced the view that outside forces could not promote democracy, and that to put this at the top of the US foreign-policy agenda was a dangerous move. Second, the association with Iraq made the democracy agenda vulnerable to the charge that its promotion was only a byword for regime change by military force – that is, for war. The association of the Iraq war with democracy promotion has become a key obstacle for the US agenda in the Middle East (Speck, 2006). It has diminished support, at home and abroad, for American democracy initiatives, and has made it easy for those hostile to them to dismiss them as a unviable policy. Given the ongoing security crisis in Iraq, it has become much harder to argue that the US could play a positive role in the promotion of democracy in the wider Middle East and in North Africa.

Arab criticisms of US foreign policy post-9/11

The Bush administration's democratic programme led to criticism not only in US foreign-policy circles but also in the Arab world. All political quarters, from right to left and including Islamists in the region, were critical and greeted the US agenda with defiance (Ottaway, 2003). A statement by Condoleezza Rice (the then US Secretary of State) provoked anger and a quick response from the Arab press, expressing discontent with the US's sudden concern for the political situation in the Middle East. Rice had declared that the US was committed not only to the removal of Saddam Hussein but also to 'the democratisation or the march of freedom in the Muslim world' (*Financial Times*, 23 September 2002). The Jordanian daily *Al-Dustour* replied that there are 'more than one and a half billion Muslims who suffer from American greed and oppression and from its cruel and visible war against Islam and Muslims'. The London-based *Al-Hayat* lashed out against 'Ayatollah Condoleezza and the Export of Democracy' (Middle

East Media and Research Institute, 11 October 2002). Rice's statement led Arab analysts to conclude that the US planned to remove
what it classed as 'rogue states' in the Middle East, in order to
impose its vision of democracy on the region.

As a result, for various commentators the US promotion of
democracy in the Middle East became synonymous with what they
saw as its imperial designs and ambitions in the region. Husayn
Abd-al-Wahid, of the Egyptian newspaper *Akhbar al-Yawm*,
declared (31 August 2002):

> Within this framework, the only logical explanation for the
> so-called US programme for bolstering democracy in the
> Middle East is that it is merely a means of pressuring Arab
> and Islamic governments and regimes to become more
> cooperative with US policies on Palestine, Iraq and Sudan,
> Afghanistan and other areas where Washington is commit-
> ting gross mistakes that worry everybody.

Islamic leaders in the Middle East have continuously played
the anti-imperialist card to resist American democracy initiatives
in the region. Islamists were adamant that the US would never
permit the holding of truly free and fair elections because of the
possibility of political parties coming to power that are adverse
to US interests in the region. Azzam Huneidi, head of the MB's
political front in Jordan, the IAF, has stated:

> America is calling for reform. But would America be happy
> with the results of free and clean elections? No, they would
> not be happy. They want the results they want. A recent
> public opinion survey in Jordan indicated that 99% of the
> people hate America. If there were truly free elections, the
> results would be a parliament that hated America. What
> the US wants is democracy according to American stand-
> ards. (Wickham, 2004: 3)

Raheil Gharaybeh, also a member of the IAF, stated: 'This is what the Arab people think. Real democracy will hurt American interests. Any real reforms will work against Israel and America' (Wickham, 2004: 4). Mohammad Mahdi Akef, the supreme guide of the MB in Egypt between 2004 and 2010, declared: 'The Muslim Brotherhood rejects all shapes of foreign hegemony, and denounces foreign interference in the affairs of Egypt or any other Arab or Islamic country' (*Islam Online*, 4 March 2004).

The Bush administration's lack of credibility did not help its democratisation programme. The US is viewed as championing the ideals of democracy and freedom while at the same time supporting the policies of the Israeli state, which occupies Palestinian territories. 'This superpower, which protects and sponsors Sharon's mass killings and systematic destruction of Palestinian life, cannot emerge as an "angel" in Lebanon, calling for virtuous work and looking after the seeds of democracy,' argues Talal Salam, a Lebanese writer (*Al Safir*, 9 September 2002). Fahd Fanek, of the *Jordan Times*, argued along the same lines when he stated (30 September 2002): '[A]nd what does Bush have to say about the so-called Israeli democracy, which has produced the worst kind of far-right extremist government…?'

A further dent in the Bush administration's credibility was the small budget it set aside for its policy of promoting democracy in the Middle East. 'The US has set aside no more than $30 million to support freedom and support democracy in the Arab region,' commented *Al-Quds Al-Arabi* newspaper (*Middle East Mirror*, 18 November 2002). A writer in Qatar added: 'Allocating $29 million is not even enough to launch an advertising campaign in the United States for a local domestic product' (*Middle East Mirror*, 18 November 2002). This small allocation of funds was seen by the Arab press as a clear indication that the Bush administration had no real interest in promoting democracy in the Middle East.

It is clear that the US democratisation agenda has come under much criticism in the post-9/11 Middle East. To win internal support for its programme the US needs to take a number of steps. For example, it should remove the double standards apparent in its foreign policy, develop a more balanced position on the Arab-Israeli conflict, and consult with internal political actors, both secular and Islamist, in the context of democracy promotion. These basic steps are important if the US is to win support in the region for its programme. However, so far US policy-failures post-9/11 (e.g. Guantanamo Bay, Abu Ghraib, extraordinary rendition and allegations of torture) are not helping in its policy to promote democracy in the region (Bayet, 2003). There clearly needs to be a revision of that policy for it to win any legitimacy and credibility in its push for democracy in the Middle East.

The election of President Barack Obama was seen as a chance for change in US behaviour and policy positions in the region. Obama withdrew troops from Iraq, showed support for the Saudi initiative to solve the Palestinian-Israeli crisis and also spoke of his desire to close Guantanamo Bay, a disaster for US public relations in the Middle East, which were positive gestures and positions. However, Obama's position on Pakistan, where he has escalated military operations in the tribal areas, has dented his administration's reputation in the Muslim world, and the extent to which he is willing to push key allies such as Egypt, Jordan and Saudi Arabia to change and reform will be a yardstick for Obama's democratic credentials in the region.

Conclusion

This chapter has explored the process of economic and political change in the Middle East, taking into consideration the impact of any process of political change on state powers and structures. In particular it has considered the role of Islamist parties and the challenge which they have mounted to state power, facilitated by the fact that Islamists were present both inside and outside the system, and by their existence in and engagement with civil society via their involvement in trade unions, professional syndicates, student unions and teaching clubs, all of which gave them a strong position from which to challenge state power in the Middle East. This challenge continued post-9/11, with Islamists becoming more central to politics in the region. Examining their position provides a basis from which to look at the role of external actors in the process of political change. US post-9/11 foreign policy has in turn been examined, to deduce the extent to which it has been inclusive of democracy promotion in the Middle East. This gives an understanding of the prospects for political reform in the region and sets a framework within which to examine the process of economic and political change in Egypt.

3

CRISIS AND CHANGE: ECONOMIC AND POLITICAL REFORM IN EGYPT

This chapter explores the process of economic and political reform in Egypt after 1991, to investigate in particular whether there was any substantial impact on the power and the authoritarian structure of the state. Looking at the economic situation in Egypt and the factors which led to the government's economic reform from 1991, this provides a backdrop to the exploration of economic and political change in Egypt.

Background: from economic crisis to economic reform

Modern Egyptian history shows a cyclical transition of growth patterns post-1952, in addition to several radical economic and political transformations (Al Sayid, 2003). Starting from the 1952 military coup d'état, the new government overhauled the previous economic system, impacting the whole of society. The adoption of a planned-economy approach meant that the Egyptian officers in charge established a public sector, extensive nationalisation and a widespread process of income redistribution, accompanied by a series of important social policies (Waterbury, 1983; Woodward,

1992). The early stages following the 1952 revolution were char-acterised by political challenges and resistance to Nasser's rule, which affected economic development and the levels of economic growth (Stephens, 1973; Ayubi, 1995). First, from 1952 to 1954 there was a challenge to Nasser from the political opposition, in particular from the Islamic movement led by the MB (*Al Ahram*, 27 June–3 July 2002; Hopwood, 1993). Second, Nasser also faced political challenges from inside the Free Officers movement, who were unhappy with the concentration of power and resources in Nasser's hands. Once he was able to deal with the internal and external challenges, however, Egypt improved economically, from the mid-1950s to the mid-1960s; but from 1967 until approxi-mately 1973 Egypt fell into an economic crisis, which was made worse by the heavy involvement of the Egyptian army in Northern Yemen (1962–67) and the heavy military losses sustained in the 1967 Six Days War against Israel (O'Brien, 2002; Aboul Enien, January/February 2004; Dresch, 2000).

The 1973 conflict with Israel was a turning point for Egypt, whose success in this war raised Sadat's political and social legiti-macy, allowing him to step out of Nasser's shadow. As a result Sadat introduced the *Infitah*, a process of economic liberalisation, which led Egypt to undergo a change of economic model – a transition from a state-led to a market economy. This transition had severe socio-economic implications for Egypt (Aoude, 1994; Beattie, 2000; Sullivan, 1990; Ayubi, 1991; 1988). According to the WB, 'malnutrition increased between 1978 and 1986, partic-ularly among school children' (1991: 66). The underprivileged of Egypt – with minimal job opportunities and skills, depended on the Egyptian state and its welfare system for much-needed socio-economic services such as subsidies, education and health, but this changed with the *Infitah*, as the state began to marketise and reduce its economic activity (El-Laithy, 1997: 147; see also Harik, 1997: 21). The economic liberalisation policies of the *Infitah* were disastrous in that they widened the gap between rich and poor.

What was also troubling was the rise of a parasitic element to the economy, which was closely associated with the state and was prospering through the use of illegal means to secure its economic objectives. These underhanded channels would take its toll on the Egyptian economy, and caused a strain on the mircro-economic level due to a number of unproductive operations that left essential construction and development projects uncompleted and so added to the infrastructural-development crisis in which Egypt found itself.

Moreover, the Egyptian economy's problems began to weaken it at the macro-economic level. Egypt's total external debt in 1977 was over US$5.7 billion, 42 per cent of its GNP (World Bank, 2000). It was also suffering weak economic growth, and a severe budget deficit of over US$2 billion. This micro- and macro-economic crisis led the Egyptian government in 1976 to begin its first discussions with the International Monetary Fund (IMF) on an economic rescue package. This led to a US$450 million loan, contingent on Egypt's willingness to implement economic measures such as currency reform and reductions in government expenditure on social and welfare services (Abdelazim, 2002). As a result of these negotiations, Egyptian policy-makers took the risky decision of vowing to reduce state expenditure by cutting subsidies. However, when the government cut bread subsidies, a much-needed food commodity, the results were disastrous: the 1977 bread riots (Ahmed et al, 2001). These riots posed a major danger to Egypt's social and political stability (IMF, 1996; 2001). However, as Egypt's domestic socio-economic problems worsened, the government tried to solve them with short- and long-term loans, finding itself in November 1977 in negotiations for a US$600 million loan from the IMF over a three-year period, rather than the US$450 million. The IMF allowed Egypt to withdraw only US$105 million in 1977, because it was worried that excessive borrowing would lead the country to exceed its ability to repay (El Gafarawi, 1999). Meanwhile, however, the US was worried that a lack of available funds would lead Egypt into further domestic insecurity; consequently it pushed the IMF to allow Egypt to borrow more (Rivlin, 1985: 179–80).

However, the IMF's conditions for Egypt's borrowing ignored the socio-economic fallout from tightening fiscal and monetary policy. For the government, however, this fallout was critically important, and its main objective was thus to seek a compromise between external pressure and internal stability (Abdelazim, 2002). As result, the government continued to deal with the IMF and WB, seeking new loans and abiding by their conditions but at the same time taking account of the socio-economic consequences and their impact on political stability (Harik, 1997: 105; Clark, 2000: 161).

The Egyptian economy from the 1980s to 1991

At the core of Egypt's macro-economic crisis in the 1980s were three main imbalances. First, there was a gap between domestic savings and investment; second, imports exceeded exports; and third, government spending exceeded revenues. A number of factors contributed to these macro-economic imbalances. First, the collapse of oil revenues and the mounting losses of public-sector companies undermined public savings (Richards, 1991; 2001; Richards and Waterbury, 1990; 1996; Handoussa and Potter, 1991). Second, private savings were limited, as a result of uncertainty on the part of private wealth-holders as to the future direction and credibility of economic policy, resulting in capital flight from Egypt. Third, investment flowed into infrastructure rather than into the production of traded goods, and investment was too low to lead to the creation of enough jobs to absorb the vast number of unemployed within Egyptian society (Richards and Waterbury, 1990; Handoussa and Potter, 1991).

Also, at the macro-economic level – because of excessive borrowing under Sadat and then Mubarak – Egypt's foreign debt became a nagging problem, climbing from approximately US$2 billion in 1970 to some US$21 billion in 1980 (El Gafarawi, 1999). This huge rise was a direct result of state borrowing undertaken to plug the saving-investment gap within the economy. By 1988 total external debt was expected to reach US$46 billion, or more than double the 1980 level. As a result, in 1987 civilian debt came close to GDP, and in 1988 surpassed it (Richards, 1991; 2001). Most of Egypt's debt was owed to other governments, or guaranteed by them, especially when military debt was taken into account. For example, in 1987 debt to private creditors was about 21 per cent and to multilateral organisations about 17 per cent of the civilian total. Prior to the peace treaty with Israel in 1979, the largest creditors were Arab countries; after that date the Organisation for Economic Co-operation and Development (OECD) members replaced Arabs. In 1987 Egypt owed US$10.1 billion to the US (Richards, 1991; 2001), of which about US$4.6 billion – or some 23 per cent of the country's combined debt – was military-related. In Egypt itself, the largest debtors were the government and the public sector: public debt, not counting the military component, made up about 78 per cent of the total, the rest being borne by private enterprises. As new foreign lending dried up in the latter part of the 1980s, the deficit began to be financed by monetary expansion. Inflation, as a result of an increase in the money supply, rose, affecting living standards within Egypt. From 1976 to 1986 the consumer price index rose from 164.2 to 708.8 in urban areas and from 187.8 to 795.8 in rural areas (Oweiss, 1990). Over the same period the national inflation rate itself generally increased, growing from 10.3 per cent in 1976 to 23.9 per cent in 1986 (*World Guide*, 2001/02).

Egypt's economy began the 1990s with chronic macro- and micro-problems, including a growing fiscal deficit, an escalating inflation rate, worsening balance of payment deficits and declining international reserves. For example, real GDP growth decreased from 3.9 per cent in the fiscal year 1987/88 to 2.3 percent in 1990/91, and the Egyptian pound was devalued from 1.761 to

3.009 per US dollar (Abdel Khalek 1992; 1993; Kienle and Spring, 1998). At the micro level the quality of governmental services, such as health, transport and education, had dropped, which directly impacted on the state, as the provision of such services underpinned the legitimacy of the post-colonial Egyptian state.

The Gulf War in 1991 did not help Egypt's suffering economy. Iraq's invasion of Kuwait in August 1990 and the subsequent war (February 1991) vastly reduced Egypt's economic resources. The war also forced the return of 700,000 workers from the Gulf countries and a severe decline in tourism. Adding to these difficulties, the servicing of Egypt's debt, which now totalled US$46 billion, became an imminent threat to the economy (*Economist*, 25 October 1997; see also World Bank, 2000). In reply to the growing socio-economic problems, the Egyptian government turned to the IMF, as it had done in 1976, 1978 and 1987. The Egyptian government adopted a conventional stabilisation and structural adjustment package, endorsed by the IMF in exchange for massive debt relief (Bush, 1999; 2004; Licari, 1997). Such a bargain was attractive to the Egyptian regime economically and politically. Economically, the reduction of up to US$20 billion of debt reduced annual interest payments by US$12 billion over the next ten years. Politically, the economic rescue package was easier to sell domestically since the government could argue that debt relief would greatly help the ailing Egyptian economy, and that international creditors were acknowledging part responsibility for past mistakes. Another incentive was that the IMF was ready to accept a somewhat more gradual approach to implementation of economic reform, as it recognised Egypt's key geopolitical and strategic role in the region (Shafiq, 1998). The structure and organisation underpinning the Egyptian economy in the 1980s and early 1990s were fragile. The government's adoption of economic reform in 1991 was a direct result of the ailing fortunes of the Egyptian economy. These reforms heralded a new dawn for the Egyptian state, and it is important to understand this programme

– in particular its rationale, objectives and impact. The following discussion of the programme will allow a platform from which to explore the process of economic and political change in Egypt.

Economic reform, 1991

Egypt had undertaken a number of agreements with the IMF to alleviate its socio-economic problems (IMF, 2001); it signed three stand-by agreements, in 1976, 1978 and 1987, which followed the same line of policy recommendations as would be outlined in the 1991 agreement. All three agreements were discontinued for primarily socio-economic reasons (*Economist*, 25 October 1997). The development of inherent economic problems in Egypt, such as huge levels of debt (reaching US$50 billion in June 1990) resulted in the opening of a new set of economic negotiations with the IMF (Abdel Khalek, 1992; Lofgren, 1993). A stand-by agreement was concluded in May 1991, the implementation of the economic stabilisation programme having started even earlier, on 1 January 1991 (Korayem, 1997). The plan to improve macro-economic indicators was central to the programme. The restoration of internal and external economic balances would be achieved by the implementation of demand-management policies, including the reduction and switching of expenditure, using mainly monetary and fiscal policies. The IMF's view was that macro-economic stabilisation was urgently needed, particularly in heavily indebted countries, in order to achieve long-term growth. This process included the use of monetary and fiscal policies. Abdel Khalek explains this:

> The fiscal adjustment lies at the heart of the stabilisation package and involves trimming off the fiscal deficit, both the overall and bank financed par. The target is to bring down the ratio of the overall budget deficit to GDP from an estimated high of 22 per cent for 1990/91 to a mere 1.5 per cent by 1995/96. It stipulates a slight reduction in the ratio of public expenditure to GDP, and a substantial hike in the

share of public revenue. But it is interesting to note that in relative terms, central government non-tax revenue will provide most of the targeted adjustment, namely through price increases, particularly in energy prices. The increase in tax revenue is mainly through greater reliance on indirect taxation. (1992: 44–5)

The outline macro-economic objective of the programme was gradually to reduce inflation, down to 5 per cent by 1994/95. The investment ratio was expected to rise from 19.5 per cent of GDP in 1990/91 to 24.6 per cent in 1995/96. To achieve this rise, there was to be strong emphasis on the private sector and its development. Public investment outlays were to fall from about 15 per cent of GDP in 1990/91 to less than 8.5 per cent in 1996/97. The saving rate was targeted to rise from an average of 9.4 per cent of GDP in 1990/91 to 16.9 per cent in 1995/96 (El Gafarawi, 1999). As a result of this economic programme, real growth in output was expected gradually to recover, reaching 3 per cent or more by 1994/19. The second component of the economic programme was the process of structural adjustment, which included a set of economic reforms and regulations to promote a fundamental change in the ownership structure and organisation of the Egyptian economy. It contained three main policy areas: price liberalisation, trade liberalisation and investment reform (El Gafarawi, 1999). Investment reform included public-sector restructuring, privatisation and improving the investment environment for private activities.

The economic programme was planned to be implemented through various phases, under the auspices of the IMF and the WB (Seddon, 1990). By the mid-1990s two phases had been completed, with a third in progress. The first agreement with the IMF was signed in May 1991 – an 18-month stand-by agreement – but this had to be extended to March 1993, with US$278 million of Special Drawing Rights (SDRs) (El Gafarawi, 1999). The second was the Extended Fund Facility arrangement, in September 1993.

The signing of the first stand-by agreement with the IMF had shortly been followed by a structural adjustment loan from the WB, in June 1993. The WB went on to support the second phase, and the reform programme was also backed by other foreign creditors, such as the African Development Bank (Korayem, 1997). In the case of Egypt the use of cross-conditionality was clear, and the IMF imposed stricter conditions on Egypt so that implementation of the agreement would proceed according to the plan. Both the IMF and the WB divided the disbursement of their credit into two tranches, relating the release of each to the fulfilment of reform measures. Before each disbursement IMF or WB officials would visit Egypt to review the previous phase with the Egyptian government, and to set the performance criteria for the following phase. To ensure Egypt met these criteria the IMF and WB conducted extensive monitoring.

The second tranche, due in November 1992, was not released until May 1993. The delay was a result of the IMF's perception that the pace of reform was too slow, and that some of the economic objectives which had been set could not be achieved within the scheduled time. There was dissatisfaction with the progress of the privatisation programme, and the Egyptian government tried to correct this by announcing its first major privatisation programme in February 1993 (Korayem, 1997). The signing of the agreement, its nature and the actors involved can be deduced from the above, but it is more important to explore the impact of economic reform. It was this that had a key bearing on the process of political reform and on the Egyptian government's subsequent political strategy during the 1990s.

The Egyptian government was taking new steps towards achieving long-term macro-economic stabilisation and strengthening the financial sector. The objectives were to unify exchange rates, raise interest rates, bring energy prices up to world levels over five years, raise taxes, eliminate most consumer subsidies over five years, pursue privatisation and reduce the budget deficit (Clark,

2000). It is generally assumed that the government managed to reduce the deficit in the state budget. Government investment as a percentage of GDP was reduced from 13.5 per cent in 1990/91 to only 5.5 per cent in 1995/96, and the subsidy outlay was reduced from 5.9 per cent of GDP to 1.9 per cent over the same period. Measures to increase revenues focused mainly on the increase in levels of taxation, and resulted in the imposition of a new sales tax, replacing the consumption tax, and a stamp tax in addition, to a unified income tax. The economic programme reduced the level of inflation, official figures indicating a reduction from 21.1 per cent in 1991/19 to 7.2 per cent in 1995/96.

With regard to the exchange rate, the former multiple-exchange-rate system was replaced by a single-rate, market-orientated system, with a managed floating of the Egyptian pound for all public and private transactions (Kamar and Bakardzhieva, 2003). Although the Egyptian pound depreciated during 1991, the exchange rate stabilised in a range between LE3.35–3.45 to the US dollar from the third quarter of 1991 until the fourth quarter of 1998. Foreign reserves increased significantly, from only US$3.6 billion in 1990/91 to US$21.1 billion in 1997/98, an increase of more than 500 per cent. The real GDP growth-rate, meanwhile, declined sharply in the first two-year period of the economic reform programme, from 2.5 per cent to 1.9 per cent. However, after 1993, the rate grew steadily, reaching 5.7 per cent in 1997/98 (El Mahdi, 1997).

The IMF itself praised the Egyptian government for its achievements in the context of macro-economic stabilisation (IMF, 1996). According to an IMF press release in 1996, Egypt improved public finances and made major advances in decentralising its economy:

> Real GDP growth accelerated to over 4 percent in 1995/96 from virtual stagnation in 1991/92, while the rate of inflation declined to 7 percent from over 21 percent. The overall balance of payments remained in surplus, leading

to a substantial accumulation of net international reserves. With limited external borrowing and further debt relief from the Paris Club, the ratio of external debt GDP fell to 47 percent in mid 1996 from about 75 percent in 1991/92, and the debt service ratio declined to about 11 percent of current account receipts from 14 percent in 1991/92. (No. 95/50, 11 October 1996)

To facilitate the process of structural adjustment of the Egyptian economy some important legislative measures were introduced, with a view to establishing a capital market in the country and removing price distortions in many sectors. In the agricultural sector Law 96 was introduced in 1992, ending fixed rents for culti-vated land (Bush, 2002; 2004). Legislative measures were intro-duced aimed at providing a proper institutional framework for the new liberal economic policies. The most important of these measures included the Law of the Public Sector (103 of 1991), which allowed privatisation of public-sector companies, the Law of Capital Markets (92 of 1993), the Law of Exchange (38 of 1994) and the Law of Lease Financing (95 of 1995).

However, the structural-adjustment phase of the economic reforms was criticised by the IMF, which stated that Egypt had failed to achieve the level of economic reform the IMF had expected (IMF, 1996). The IMF was critical in particular of the pace of public-sector privatisation, which had slowed in the later 1990s. Despite important steps taken by the Egyptian government to privatise small units in the state-owned sector, large indus-trial complexes, particularly in textiles, steel and capital goods, in general remained in government hands. Public enterprises continued to account for as much as a third of Egypt's manu-facturing sector, half of its investment expenditure and about 15 per cent of total employment (IMF, 1996). It thus became clear that the Egyptian state remained unwilling to weaken its control over the economic sector, and this because of an economic and political logic. First, to the Egyptian state, the movement of capital into private hands was viewed as weakening its economic power. Second, such a movement was perceived as weakening the state's ability to co-opt, thus its political power. Given the importance of privatisation in understanding economic and political change, it is necessary to explore in more detail the privatisation experience in Egypt.

After 1991, the Egyptian government started an extensive programme of privatising state-owned enterprises (SOEs). Since 1991 economic reform has been focused on privatising public-sector companies. A number of factors were behind this privatisation drive, such as the public deficits caused by the SOE sector, and severe economic problems such as inflation and the obstruction of export growth (Waterbury, 1992: 183). Although the government originally called this programme 'reform and privatisation', its main goal was to privatise SOEs (Abdelazim, 2002). While the declared goal of this programme was to reform many of these SOEs, in fact the real aim was to improve their financial situation by decreasing and settling their debts, thus preparing them for privatisation. The government introduced two main methods of privatising SOEs. (El Gafarawi, 1999). The first focused on improving their management by allowing managers to work independently of their respective ministries. The 1991 SOE Law facilitated this, in that it gave economic enterprises more control over issues such as management, budgets, pricing and funding. However, employment and suspension continued to be supervised and dictated by government regulations and bureaucracy (see Waterbury, 1992; Mohieldin and Nasr, 1996).

A second method went hand in hand with the selling process itself. It allowed the Egyptian government to offer most of the SOEs for sale following a medium-term schedule; this approach meant that these would move from the state's hands to the private sector. (Abdelazim, 2002). Those SOEs which faced financial problems were dealt with according to the first method, and the more attractive ones according to the second. Despite these two procedures outlined by the government, the process of privatisation did not proceed as quickly as it had planned. According to the US Department of Commerce:

> In January 1997, the government announced its plan ... to privatise 33 companies through anchor investor sales and 12 companies in Initial Public Offerings (IPOs). In the first five months of 1997, only six companies were privatised through Egypt's ... LE60.3 billion ($17.8 billion) stock market. Only one company was sold to an anchor investor in the same time period. At this rate, the government may not be able to meet its 1997 objectives for privatisation. (Galal and Tohamy, 1994: 28; see also NTDB, 1997)

The point to be noted here is that Egyptian decision-makers, despite experimenting with different methods of privatisation, have not had a specific plan or strategy for implementing it (Abdelazim). This became particularly clear during the second batch of sales, which used three methods of selling (Mohieldin and Nasr, 1996: 43–6). The first was selling to an 'anchor' investor who bought all the company's shares. The government sold three companies in this: Pepsi Cola Bottling, El Nasr Coca Cola Bottling and El Nasr Steam Boiler Manufacturing; having done so, it has since preferred not to sell any further public companies to such anchor investors, as it wants to avoid creating monopolies (Mohieldin and Nasr, 1996: 43–5).

To accelerate the process, the Cabinet Privatisation Committee, headed by then Prime Minister Atif Obeid, decided to privatise a number of profitable companies, including some in tourism, maritime transport, cement, fertiliser and tobacco production (Abdelazim, 2002). The general consensus is that the stock in five-star hotels and in the Eastern Tobacco Company has been the most attractive investments in the privatisation process (*Al*

Ahram, 7–13 December 2000). The Egyptian Maritime Transport Company was sold to Egyptian investors, and paved the way for the sale of the Alexandria Shipyard Company and the Egyptian Ship Repair Company (*Al Ahram*, 7–13 December 2000). After several years of a drive to speed up the privatisation process, during which 180 firms with a total value of LE5.8 billion were sold, the pace started to slow once again. In 2001 only 13 transactions took place, down from 23 in 2000 and 33 in 1999. This was mainly due to the fact that most well-performing companies had already been sold, and the remainder were either heavily indebted, over-staffed, using outdated machinery or in need of radical restructuring. However, three other major factors also acted as key obstacles to the Egyptian state undergoing comprehensive privatisation of SOEs in the 1990s (Aoude, 1994). These were:

- the capitalist bureaucracy sought to maintain the public sector, in which it had vested interests;
- private capital was reluctant to invest, given excessive bureaucracy and weak legal infrastructure; and
- privatisation would heighten socio-economic problems. A large number of workers are employed in SOEs, so reduction in employment would lead to worker discontent – the selling of SOEs in Egypt has led to numerous riots and demonstrations. It is reported that strikes rose from eight in 1990 to 26 in 1991, 28 in 1992 and 63 in 1993. In a major strike at Kafr al Dawwar in September 1994, three people were shot dead by the police, and many others subsequently injured. This kind of civil unrest was conducive to social and political instability, which the Egyptian government feared (Kienle and Spring, 1998).

These three factors obstructed the process of privatisation, and therefore structural adjustment in Egypt. The government sought the right balance between macro-economic stabilisation and structural adjustment to try to meet both the pressures of the IFIs and internal socio-economic demands. However, it was clear by the 1990s that despite its balancing act the state had failed to meet internal socio-economic demands, and the result was crisis. This would have severe implications for the process of political change and for the government's political strategy.

The rate of unemployment rose throughout the 1980s; the official estimate in the 1986 population census was 10 per cent, while that of the Labour Force Sample Survey (LFSS) was between 9 and 10 per cent. A better estimate, which took into account those who became discouraged from searching for work because of the high level of unemployment, raised the rate to 17 per cent. However, some academic studies put the level even higher, to about 20 per cent (Fergany, 1998). According to WB data, unemployment in Egypt in 1994 was 17.4 per cent; and more than 70 per cent of those unemployed were less than 20 years old. It is a common experience, found in other countries that have undertaken economic reform, that negative impacts on employment are frequent, especially in the short term (Korayem, 1997). The problem was made even more severe in Egypt when in 1986 the government abandoned its policy of guaranteeing state employment in the public sector to fresh university graduates.

The restrictive fiscal and monetary policies advocated by the economic programme affected the poor by eliminating their social safety net. Through the abolition or reduction of subsidies for basic consumer commodities, the poor had to pay a substantial amount more to acquire basic food commodities such as bread and rice. As the WB noted, subsidy programmes as a proportion of GDP dropped by more than 11 per cent between 1982 and 1995 (World Bank, 1995). For example, 'the commodity coverage of food subsidies has been restricted to popular bread, a limited quantity of edible oil, and sugar' (Kheir El Din, 1996: 1). By 1995, levels of government investment had been reduced by two-thirds since the mid-1980s (World Bank, 1996), when:

Five basic commodities (sugar, rice, edible oil, tea and soap) were subsidized by LE 1,390 million in 1986/87. Ten million Egyptians held family coupons from the Ministry of Supply that entitled them to a fixed quota of these goods at subsidized prices (Harik, 1997: 97).

This distributional system to an extent guaranteed that these subsidised foods and commodities found their way to the most vulnerable people in Egypt (El Gafarawi, 1999). The centralised state, represented by the Ministry of Supply, had secured these minimum staples for the poor, but after the introduction of structural adjustment policies 'the Ministry of Supply abolished the quota distribution system, except for ordinary and patent flour, which is consumed in the production of subsidized bread, and edible oil and sugar, which were distributed through ration cards' (Nassar and Fawzy, July/October 1993: 56). Education and health services were clearly also important contributors to human development, but during the period of economic reform funding for education and health was reduced considerably. One academic study estimated that government expenditure on education as a percentage of total expenditure fell from 16.7 percent in 1970/71 to 10 per cent in 1989/90 (El Gafarawi, 1999). The health sector experienced the same reduction in expenditure, and a consequent deterioration in services and facilities. Government expenditure on health, as a proportion of its total expenditure, declined from 4.8 per cent in 1970/71 to 1.9 percent in 1989/90.

The extent of poverty in Egypt increased rapidly during the 1980s; it continued to increase in the 1990s, but more slowly up to the middle of the decade. In 1996 around 13.7 million Egyptians lived below the international poverty line of one US dollar per day (Al Sayid, 2003). Egypt's poverty profile reveals that the poor are usually either occupied in marginal activities and low-wage work, or are unemployed, in both urban and rural areas. Most are illiterate or have very little education. Although there has been some progress, this itself is not satisfactory, either because the pace of development is very slow, or because in some areas setbacks have emerged, such as an increase in malnourished children. Moreover, a large proportion of the rural population are still deprived of basic social services, as a result of the state's economic contraction, due in turn to economic reform.

It is apparent that the Egyptian government failed to meet internal socio-economic demands, with economic reform (i.e. macro-economic stabilisation and structural adjustment) leading to a socio-economic crisis. The situation of the majority of Egyptians deteriorated rapidly during the period of economic reform in the 1990s. The uneven nature of the impact resulted in the balance of power in society between rich and poor widening: the business class who championed the direction and extent of economic reform were able to benefit from limited privatisation and trade liberalisation, maintaining their control over public companies and the latter's monopolisation of economic sectors. Given the growing socio-economic crisis and heightened social unrest, what was required was a safety net, to cushion the masses from the worst of the socio-economic damage. The Egyptian government had quickly to find a solution if it was to maintain any sense of legitimacy, with the market having excluded many of those it governed.

The concept of a social safety-net was thought of by the Egyptian government as a way of solving the heightened socio-economic crisis in the country. The key objective was to compensate the most vulnerable groups, particularly those harmed by structural adjustment and the consequent shrinking of the subsidies system (Kheir el Din, 1996). The idea of such a safety net became popular with those advocating neo-liberal economic reforms in the 1980s, as a means of providing a 'human face' in the midst of growing socio-economic crisis. Ghana was one of the first countries to put this idea into effect: in 1987, realising the socio-economic costs of its structural-adjustment programme, the Ghanaian government introduced a 'Programme of Action to Mitigate the Social Consequences of Adjustment' (PAMSCAD) (ODI, July 1996). Since then a number of programmes and policies targeted at poverty reduction have been introduced in Ghana, some with a limited mandate targeted at a specific vulnerable group (Sowa, 2002). To provide this 'human face' the Egyptian government established in 1991 a 'Social Fund for Development' (SFD) to alleviate the growing socio-economic crisis, during the various phases of macro-economic stabilisation and structural adjustment. One of the SFD's mandates when initially established was to support the government's economic reform and structural-adjustment programme, and to work as:

> social safety nets to protect those most vulnerable to the adverse effects of the reform programme. Measures were to be developed to assist unemployed and displaced workers, all within the government's fiscal targets – either through the commitment of new funds, or through the reallocation of existing subsidies or transfer funds. The adverse effects of economic restructuring on workers were to be minimised through this social safety net (Social Fund for Development, 1999: 12).

The Egyptian government promised $1.1 billion to the SFD, but it failed to meet this commitment; consequently the SFD did not have the financial resources to solve the ensuing crisis in Egypt. To compensate for this obvious shortcoming the government turned to Non-Governmental Organisations (NGOs), and began to highlight their role in providing socio-economic services at a time of economic reform. With the NGOs entering the limelight here, it is important to explore this sector, in the context of the process of economic and political change in Egypt – in particular the impacts, if any, of economic reform on NGO-state relations, and subsequently on the process of political change in Egypt.

Economic contraction – the Egyptian state and the rise of Egyptian NGOs

The rise of NGOs as economic-service providers in Egypt in the 1990s can be traced to the market policies advocated by the IMF and WB. Both actors were instrumental in promoting the process of economic liberalisation, deregulation and privatisation in Egypt (Clark, 2000). This process in essence meant the economic withdrawal of the Egyptian state from the provision of socio-economic services. This provision, leading to the construction of a social contract, has been slowly eroded under the successive regimes of Sadat and Mubarak, although it is fair to make the point that the erosion escalated under the latter, as a result of economic reform in 1991 (Bayat, 2003; Gutner, 1999). Thus NGOs became central actors in the provision of socio-economic services in Egypt in the 1990s (Chiriboga, 2002; Michael, 2002).

The NGO capacity to act as an effective social safety-net in Egypt varied from time to time and place to place – no generalisation can be made about their performance. Their ability to replace the state as it withdrew from economic activity involved two inter-related factors (Clark, 2000). The first was the service capacity and sustainability of the NGOs themselves. The second was political, that is, whether NGOs as service providers were given the political space from which to emerge, and then in which to operate. These factors need to be discussed, as they will allow an understanding of the impact of economic reform on NGO-state relations and the process of political change in Egypt.

First, in the face of the rising socio-economic problems in the country, NGOs had neither the service capacity nor the sustainability to address the needs of the increasing number of the poor in society (Clark, 2000). Egyptian NGOs on many occasions did not have the financial means or the personnel to intervene in providing much-needed socio-economic services. Second, the work of the NGO sector in Egypt was obstructed by the fact that the government failed to withdraw politically. This meant that the

NGOs, as service providers, were not given the political space in which to function. This is in turn was because the Egyptian state post-1952 had become accustomed to comprehensive control and power, through the introduction of restrictive laws and legislation, and in particular of corporatist structures and relationships. Corporatism reached its peak under Nasser, in the context of his larger programme of socialism and nationalisation (Pratt, 2004; Abdel Rahman, 2004). Nasser restructured group activity in each occupation into new corporatist groups, producing a political system under state control. Sadat and Mubarak then reshaped the corporatist structures they inherited into more reliable instruments of control and co-option. The process of corporatism has therefore been a source of control and inevitably of power; actors beyond the control of the state were not permitted, in case they developed power to challenge the hegemony of the state. In this post-1952 context of survival, power and hegemony, the performance and behaviour of NGOs has been monitored and checked through restrictive legislation and corporatism, in case they evolved into a force capable of challenging the economic policy and decision-making process of the state (El Said, interview, 2004; El Abdel Fattah, interview, 2004). The first necessity for a state to maintain its hegemony is consensus. The NGOs' capacity to challenge this consensus, on economic policy in particular, resulted in the state keeping a close eye on them after 1952.

In Egypt, NGO–state relations and the process of political change at a time of economic reform in the 1990s needs to be viewed through the prism of corporatism, which has been exercised under Law 32 of 1964 (Clark, 2000). The existence of Law 32 had for decades restricted the NGOs' sector, and they had for a long time been calling for it to be changed. Law 32 allowed state monopoly over NGOs, requiring citizens wishing to form a voluntary organisation of any type to obtain permission from the Ministry of Social Affairs (MOSA). This permission was often denied on vague grounds, including a statement that the NGO was not needed. Once approved, an NGO had to inform MOSA of all its activities, notifying three government offices of the location and agenda of its meetings. The law also closely regulated fund-raising, allowing only membership dues and offerings given during religious services to be collected without MOSA permission. Permits for any other type of fund-raising were frequently denied or significantly delayed, including those granting permission for the receipt of the foreign funding so central to NGOs' operations (Posusney, 2005; Langhor, 2005). Without changes being made to the law the state would inevitably continue to control the establishment, expansion, functioning and administration of NGOs. As a result this affected the ability of NGOs to provide services and to challenge the economic consensus surrounding economic policy, which the state was constructing through state-controlled institutions, such as the media.

In May 1999, in reaction to growing pressure at a time of socio-economic crisis, and given the inability of NGOs as service providers to act effectively, the government enacted Law 153, intending that it should replace the restrictive Law 32 of 1964. This change was driven by two key factors. The first was the discourse of international donors on the importance of NGOs in providing much-needed socio-economic services at a time of economic reform. The second factor was that the Egyptian government hoped this change would bring recognition of its intentions with respect to the process of political reform at a time of heightened socio-economic crisis (Langhor, 2005). However, like the previous restrictive legislation the new law continued to restrict NGOs providing services, and also criminalised the political work of advocacy NGOs. The restrictions imposed, and the government's continual interference in NGO funding, resulted in Egypt's Constitutional Court abolishing Law 153 in June 2000; it was declared unconstitutional, primarily on the technical grounds that prior to its passage the necessary bodies had not approved it. In response to the striking down of this law, and the obvious embarrassment of the government, the People's Assembly passed Law 84 of 2002, the new NGO Law (*Al Ahram*, 6–12 June 2002; 7–13 November 2002). The law was initiated in reaction to the repeal of the previous Law 153, but, as previously, political restrictions on NGOs remained; as a result, access to foreign funding was further restricted. Under previous laws NGOs had been allowed to accept money, without prior MOSA permission, from foreign agencies already in the country, but with the advent of this new law all such funding required permission. The new law continued its predecessor's insistence that MOSA, not the courts, had the right to dissolve NGOs, and it allowed the ministry to freeze the funds of NGOs that joined networks of non-governmental associations, including at the international level, without MOSA permission (Langhor, 2005). Therefore, despite these changes in the law regulating NGOs, the corporatist structure involving NGOs and the state remained intact, with the latter continuing closely to regulate the work of NGOs and subsequently to act as an obstacle to political change.

However, restrictive laws and the process of corporatism have not been the only means through which NGOs have been controlled in Egypt (BBC News, 19 September 2000; Abdel Rahman, 2002). For example, ministers and bureaucrats have not been willing to relinquish power and its associated perquisites. Also, despite the process of economic reform Egypt's political elite remains fully intact, and this has blocked any substantial progress towards political reform. As a consequence, avenues to greater political participation and to advising on policy have not opened up for NGOs. Although the process by which economic reform had led to socio-economic crisis provided the opportunity for new actors (i.e. economic NGOs) to enter the social domain, to deal with the failings of the state, the NGO sector was still looked upon suspiciously by the government in case it disturbed the economic consensus by challenging its economic policies and strategies. As a result the existence of the NGO sector was accepted, but only in an autocratic framework and context. This can be seen from the fact that the government has continued to apply restrictive laws and its corporatist structure remains firmly in place, preventing NGOs from becoming independent of state control.

It is clear that 'political space' for NGOs to provide services amid on-going economic reform in the 1990s was something of a misnomer in the Egyptian context, and this lack of a defined space for NGOs has been an area of concern. According to Mohammed El-Said Said, a human-rights activist and deputy director of Al-Ahram Center for Political and Strategic Studies, the line between the Egyptian government and NGOs is fuzzy at best. According to Said there is no real civil space in which NGOs independent of the state can thrive in Egypt. He believes that civil institutions and organisations enjoying full political and economic autonomy are effectively non-existent in the country, a problem which he attributed to the 'modernity trap' (*Al Ahram*, 8–14 November 2001). As a result of this lack of defined political space, modern civil organisations and associations such as political parties, trade unions and NGOs cannot function to check and balance the economic and political power of the Egyptian state. Nabil Abdel-Fattah, a researcher at the Al-Ahram Center, also believes that the official policy of the state is tilted towards policing NGOs rather than promoting them (*Al Ahram*, 8–14 November 2001). This has been a major obstacle to the process of political change in Egypt, with the government increasing its policing of NGOs at a time of socio-economic crisis – when it felt most vulnerable to challenges, in particular to criticism of its economic reform strategy.

This fear of challenges to its economic policies led the Egyptian state to go beyond merely policing NGOs to exert excessive political control over the whole of society, reversing the limited political opening witnessed during the 1980s. This process of rolling back political opening, known as 'political deliberalisation', coincided with growing socio-economic changes which had not abated since the 1980s. This crisis exerted excessive pressure on the power and structure of the Egyptian state, leading to perceptions of great political risk by the elite, which, in reply, reacted with the introduction of a draconian political strategy; this was to have far-reaching consequences for the process of political reform in Egypt.

Economic crisis, the Egyptian state and political deliberalisation

The process of political liberalisation began in the 1970s under Sadat, but was quickly reversed after the signing of the Camp David peace accords with Israel in 1979 (Hinnebusch, 1985). However, the process resumed once again with the advent of Hosni Mubarak as President in 1981. In the early years of his presidency Mubarak spoke of administering 'democracy in doses'. He allowed the freeing of political prisoners and press criticism of government ministers. The representation of political opposition rose to a high of 20 per cent in the 1987 elections, NGOs grew in number, student unions became politically active and professional syndicates were given more room to function and operate (Kienle, 2001; Zaki, 1995). This liberalisation on Mubarak's part can be seen in the context of his search for legitimacy. On taking over the presidency, Mubarak was not a well-known figure in Egyptian society, and so to acquire legitimacy he began to talk of attractive political change. He achieved this by showing his commitment to the rule of law and by courting the political opposition. President Mubarak continued with these political ploys in the 1980s, still in search of legitimacy (Shukrallah, 1989).

However, the prospect for political reform in the 1990s took a downturn when the Egyptian state changed its political strategy, resulting in a movement towards political deliberalisation. The government began to enforce political control over society in both urban and rural areas, re-imposing constraints on political parties, student unions and the media. In 1995–96 new legislation was introduced restricting the freedom of journalists and making it easier for the state to arrest them. (However, in reaction to a fierce backlash from journalists – even pro-governmental journalists – Egyptian government had to backtrack and repeal the legislation.) From 1999 to 2002 legislation imposed new restrictions on civil society. The arrest of Saad Eddin Ibrahim sent a clear message to all leading civil-society activists, to keep quiet or face state coercion. The Egyptian Organisation for Human Rights that had operated in Egypt since 1985 was in 1998 denied a licence to operate officially, following the arrest of its founder Hafez Abu Saeda. As a result it was forced to turn down Western funding and to scale back its activities (Sorenson, 2003). This political strategy by the government diminished the level of political participation and activity in Egypt significantly during the 1990s; the result was increasing levels of state violence in the 1995 and 2000 parliamentary elections (Brownlee, 2002; Ryan, 2001; Mustafa, 1995; Rubin, 1990).

The extent of the draconian reply of the Egyptian state in the 1990s can be understood in the context of the growing socioeconomic crisis, resulting from the economic rescue package it had implemented and the growing political power of the Islamist opposition, in particular the MB, which posed a challenge to Egyptian state power (Kienle, 2001; 2004). First, the extent of the socioeconomic crisis, notably increasing levels of poverty and unemployment, had led to internal social and political dissent, which posed a severe threat to the state's power and its structures. A fear of internal riots such as the 1977 bread riots led to the government introducing draconian policies to control society (Bayat, 1998). It was this fear of a social backlash and de-legitimisation which facilitated the process of the political deliberalisation of society during the 1990s. Second, the government faced a challenge from the MB, which had evolved into a key political actor in the 1990s, and was working at all levels in Egypt. It was involved in the provision of social services, in student unions, teaching clubs, professional syndicates and parliament itself, and was thus working both inside and outside the system. This posed a major challenge to the government, in the context of its growing socio-economic problems, and became of increasing concern – to the extent that it launched a direct attack on the MB, to weaken its organisational networks and its ability to contest and challenge state power.

The state's coercive arm was thus used to attack the structure and organisation of the MB. The regime sent 54 MB members to prison in 1995, and detained thousands without charge (Brownlee, 2002). The 1995 elections are now seen as the worst of all the elections held under the Mubarak regime, with approximately 60 people killed and hundreds injured, as a result of intimidation and violence by the police and security forces. The MB itself was targeted in particular, with members being detained in the run-up to the elections. The government perceived in the MB a direct challenge to its power, hence its policy of coercion (Brownlee, 2002; Goodson and Radwan, 1997). In 2001, in its continuing campaign to weaken the MB, it closed down *Hizb al Amal* (the Labour Party) and its newspaper *Al Shaab* (Abdalla, 2003; *Arab Reform Bulletin*, December 2004). It was able to do this by capitalising on the party's agitation against a novel accused of heresy in mid-2000. However, it was clear that this was merely an excuse for the government to suppress the party, as it too was active in society and seen as a mouthpiece for the MB.

It is hard to dispute the fact that the 1990s saw a process of political deliberalisation in Egypt, as the government tightened its control over society through its constriction of political space (Brownlee, 2002; Kienle, 1998). What emerged in the 1990s was an interplay of two main factors, which forced the state's hand: first the socio-economic crisis, and second the political weight of the MB. If one is to see either of these two factors as the more important determinant of the government's deliberalisation policy, it must be the latter. This is because it was able to exert pressure on the Egyptian government through its work inside and outside the political system, and thereby to survive government coercion and continue its challenge to the power of the state. The MB emerged as a contester for state power in the 1990s, even while the government was pushing ahead with its economic reform programme and its process of political deliberalisation.

Conclusion

This chapter has explored the process of economic and political reform in Egypt since 1991, in particular its impact on the power and structure of the Egyptian state. In the 1990s the government pursued economic reform, resulting in the reduction of expenditure on much-needed socio-economic services to the people. This led to a crisis which threatened the legitimacy and survival of the state, which, as a result, introduced a policy of political deliberalisation to contain challenges to its power and its structures. Political 'breathing space' in civil society was severely restricted, resulting in the suffocation and paralysis of the opposition. However, the MB was able to escape political extinction and to continue to challenge the state, as a result of its already broad involvement in civil society. Given the importance of the MB in challenging state power in the 1990s, it is important to explore the growth and development of the MB. The organisation's ability to contest state power was strengthened through changes in its shape and character resulting from its participation in parliament and professional syndicates. This allowed the MB to position itself, during the 1990s, to contest and challenge the Egyptian government's power and authority.

4

THE BEGINNINGS OF THE BROTHERHOOD: GROWTH AND EXPANSION UNTIL THE 1970s

The period from the 1920s to the 1970s, the focus of this chapter, is key to understanding the evolution of the MB as an important political actor in Egypt. It was through this long process of development that that the group reached a point were it was able to contest and challenge the state's power and structures in the 1990s, at a time of economic crisis.

The life and experiences of Hassan Al Banna

Hassan Al Banna had a modest conservative upbringing in rural Egypt, and so was secluded from life in large urban areas such as Cairo and Alexandria. His father, Sheikh Ahmad Abd al Rahman al Banna al Sa'ati (1881–1958), combined a trade as a watch repairer with religious scholarship. As was customary in Egyptian society, Al Banna followed in his father's footsteps (*Reflections Issue*, 4 March 2005). He learnt to repair watches and acquired an elementary religious education. At the age of 12 he registered at a local state primary school but at the same time he continued to pursue a religious vocation by joining a number of Islamic groups, such as the 'Society for Moral Behaviour' and the 'Society for Preventing the Forbidden' (Mitchell, 1969; Lia, 1998; *Ikhwanweb*, 1 March

2006). These groups put pressure on fellow townspeople to observe Islamic teaching and sent letters to those they detected violating Islamic standards. However, Al Banna would not remain with such societies long, as he would be attracted by the *Hasafiya* Sufi order, which he joined when he was 13 (Esposito, 1993; 2002). The order appealed to him because it strictly observed Islamic teachings and practices. His attachment to it also made him appreciate the importance of a strong relationship between teacher and student (Gilsenan, 1967; 1973; 1985): in his memoirs Al Banna described how one of his first teachers taught him to value the emotional bond which can grow between a teacher and student.

In 1923 Al Banna moved to Cairo, which opened his eyes to life in urban areas (Dessouki, 1982) and he was shocked by the lifestyle he encountered in Cairo, witnessing gambling, materialism, the availability of alcohol, prostitution and promiscuity (Mitchell, 1969; Lia, 1998; Aboul Enein, 2003; Husani Musa, 1956). To Al Banna all of this constituted an attack on Islamic values and norms; he blamed this on the so-called 'intellectual and social liberation movement' of Egypt, the anti-religious trend at the time, which had facilitated the erosion of Islamic values in Egypt (*Ikhwanweb*, 15 March 2006). In Al Banna's view, atheists, liberal organisations, magazines, books and newspapers were working hard to promote secular ideas which weakened the influence of religion in public life. As a result of these experiences in Cairo he came to acknowledge the existence of two camps in Egypt, that of secularism and that of Islam, with the former seen as harmful to the future of the country.

To combat the spread of secularism Al Banna sought and found men who shared his concerns, at Dar al Ulum, Al Azhar, the Law College and the Salafiya library in Cairo. Among his new acquaintances was an Azhari scholar, Sheikh Yusuf al Dijwi, who had founded a society devoted to Islamic reform (Lia, 1998; Bayyumi, 1979). Al Dijwi told Al Banna that since salvation was achieved through following Islam, there was a need to promote individual Islamic reform in society; Al Banna disagreed with this, urging him to draw on the power of the Muslim world. As a result Al Banna's first idea for a programme of action involved the formation of societies under a single religious leadership, which would inspire Islamic reform in Egypt. This resulted in the establishment of the Young Men's Muslim Association (YMMA) (Aboul Enein, 2006). This religious association, formally established in November 1927, illustrates the type of reformist movement which Al Banna emulated several months later when he founded the MB. The YMMA sought to revive Muslim society through the true Islam to be found in the Qur'an. As a long-term goal the YMMA sought to revive the Islamic Caliphate (*Ikhwanweb*, 3 April 2006).

After Al Banna graduated from Dar al Ulum in 1927, he was appointed by the Ministry of Education as an Arabic-language teacher at a primary school in Ismailiya (Lia, 1998), where the socio-economic problems Al Banna had experienced in Cairo were also evident, and where these were compounded by foreign domination and exploitation. The European managers of the Suez Canal Company resided in luxurious accommodation while Egyptians lived in miserable huts. Al Banna wanted to awaken the people to the problems which existed in Ismailiya and to lead a process of reform, according to his vision of Islam. He would visit the town's three main coffee-houses, where he would regularly deliver brief talks. At the beginning Al Banna's ideas were welcomed rather cautiously by those who gathered in the coffee houses, but after a while he began to attract a regular audience. This led to some followers asking him to lead discussions in a smaller, more private setting (Rahnema, 1994; Jameelah, 1980). Thus he began to lead private talks, and it was these which brought him into contact with people who shared his vision for Ismailiya and the rest of Egypt (Ahmad, 1996). This led Al Banna to establish the MB in Ismailiya, with six Egyptian labourers, in March 1928, with the purpose of promoting true Islam (Freedman, 2004; Mitchell, 1969; Ayubi, 1991; Bayyumi, 1979).

Expansion and growth

After 1928 the MB established branches in other Canal Zone towns in the Nile Delta. Between 1929 and 1932 the movement grew – it had five branch offices by 1930, 15 by 1932 and 300 by 1938. While exact membership figures are unknown, the 300 branches probably represented between 50,000 and 150,000 members (Mitchell, 1969). Thus, in a short period of time, the MB significantly increased the number of its branches and its membership size. This can be attributed to three key factors.

The first factor important in the growth and development of the MB was that it provided services to the people, such as education for boys and girls, cheap medical care, financial help and vocational training schemes. The provision of such services brought millions of Egyptians into contact with the MB and its vision for the country. Importantly, it allowed the MB to demonstrate its ability to deliver on social and economic promises to the Egyptian population (Munson, 2001). This led commentators to describe the MB as a state within a state (*Al Ahram*, 7 July 2005). This was important as it distanced the organisation from the centric Sufistic approach to society (i.e. individual religious reform), which was a popular trend in Egypt during the early growth and development of the MB (Rahnema, 1994; Lia, 1998). At the time of socioeconomic crisis in the 1930s and 1940s, the ability of the MB to provide much-needed services added to the weight of its reputation, and so to the challenge it was able to pose to the Egyptian government.

The second factor important in the growth and development of the MB was the extensive use of the mosque (Yakran, 1998). Other than sporting events, mosques were the only places in which the government would permit large congregations to gather. Mosques were also safe from raids or obvious government interference (*Ikhwanweb*, 3 April 2006). Even the government had to abide by the rules of the mosque, given the latter's sacred role in Islam. Despite formal government control over mosques and preachers, they provided an efficient screen for the MB to recruit new members and publicise its views to large groups of people. Mosques also gave the movement's preachers an aura of respectability, which they might not have otherwise attained if they had spoken only at street rallies. Sermons within the mosque tied their call to Islam, further legitimising the movement in society. Thus mosques were critical to the successful birth, growth and development of the MB (Munson, 2001). While the MB's leaders used numerous other methods, such as street demonstrations and public rallies, to mobilise the Egyptian people, the mosque remained the primary source of mobilisation and recruitment throughout 1932–1954 (Al Ahram, 22–28 January 2004).

The third factor important in the growth and development of the MB as a force in society was the charismatic qualities of Al Banna himself. He was able to attract huge gatherings of people to his seminars and sermons, mesmerising them with his fiery speeches and emotional rhetoric (Goldberg, 1986). His personality drew in hundreds of recruits to the MB; his magnetic personality, and his ability to inspire and lead by example, were important in the growth of the MB into a nation-wide, mass-supported movement (Hussain, 1988; Bari, 1995). Many at first considered the MB a new Sufi order, because of the central role that Al Banna played in MB recruitment, organisation and planning (Mitchell, 1969; Lia, 1998), a comparison being made between Al Banna's followers and their utter devotion to him and believers in a Sufi saint. Al Banna devoted his energy to membership recruitment and private discussions of religion and moral reform, all of which were facilitated by his dynamic and charismatic personality. His popularity allowed him to act as a religious advisor to the Egyptian monarchy and government. He wrote letters to the King on matters of national importance, and sent dozens of memoranda to Egypt's prime ministers and cabinet ministers to offer advice. Al Banna's memos stressed the need to enforce Islamic law, to promote ties with the Islamic world in general and Arab countries in particular, and to support the Palestinian cause (Choubaky, interview, 2004; Hamzawy, interview, 2004). In publicised letters, he called for specific measures, such as the banning of usury, the banning of alcohol, the expansion of hospitals and clinics, the improvement of working conditions, and a minimum wage (Mitchell, 1969; Bayyumi, 1979). Thus Al Banna, through his religious role, was able to impart his reformist vision to the Egyptian monarchy and government. His ability to do this was facilitated by the MB's involvement in politics in the late 1930s, which heralded a shift from its orthodox focus on spiritual elevation to political activism, later escalated in the 1980s and 1990s (*Ikhwanweb*, 31 March 2006).

From political activism to confrontation

The MB began in the late 1920s and early 1930s as a movement concerned with the spiritual elevation of Egyptian society. However, in the late 1930s it developed a more political outlook, in reaction to socio-economic crisis and the continual spread of secularism. This began a process of change in the MB, although these changes were minimal compared to those it would undergo in the 1980s and 1990s. The MB's shift towards politics was recognised by Al Banna in the first issue of the MB weekly, *Al Nadhir*, in May 1938. According to Al Banna the appearance of this publication marked the beginning of the movement's involvement in the internal and external political struggle – the latter being the Palestinian crisis, which had by then started in the Middle East (Jankowski, 2001). The MB conference in 1939 marked the beginning of its effective political activity in Egypt, and defined the movement as, *inter alia*, a political organisation. This shift towards political activism seems to have been led by the MB's growing sense of organisational and structural power in Egypt. Al Banna's political activism became evident, for example, on a number of occasions he cooperated with Ismail Siddiqi, the Prime Minister, on the state of affairs inside Egypt, and in 1936 the MB participated in the coronation of King

Farouq (Mitchell, 1969; Lia, 1998). In 1946 Al Banna was called to the palace for a consultation on the appointment of a new prime minister. The MB's relations with the palace were helped by the fact that Al Banna did not reject constitutional life in Egypt; rather he aimed to reform it by working from within the political system. To this end his political strategy was to introduce MB representatives to parliament through elections. However, the Prime Minister, Ahmad Maher, insisted on excluding them through the falsification of election results. This was a setback for the movement, which nevertheless continued its political activism. This was aided by the socio-economic crisis in Egypt, which allowed the MB to expand its organisational and structural power. However, the government's feelings of vulnerability to a possible challenge from the MB led it to take drastic measures: the MB was banned, its members arrested and its newspapers closed down. However, these measures did not last long, as the government was by then preoccupied with World War Two (Mitchell, 1969). The movement's meetings and forums resumed, its leadership was released from prison and it continued to expand rapidly, continuing its involvement in political activism and increasing its power – though this power was later weakened as a result of the violent situation which emerged in Egypt in the 1940s.

The turn to political violence and assassination

The British colonial presence in Egypt led to resistance involving political violence and assassinations by various groups during the late 1930s and 1940s. Between 1937 and 1942 a number of groups appeared in Egypt staging attacks against British military camps. The Egyptian Zionist Organisation blew up the Antonias Palace in Cairo and assassinated the British Resident Minister in the Middle East. Between 1946 and 1949 political violence in Egypt escalated to new heights. The assassinations of Ahmad Maher, Egypt's Prime Minister and the President of *Hizb al Wafd* (The Delegation Party) created a very unstable and turbulent political climate (Lia, 1998).

In February 1945 the MB's 'Special Unit' engaged in its first operation, with its head Al Sanadi monopolising the movement's leadership. It staged attacks against British troops and Egyptian Jewish groups for their perceived cooperation with the Zionist movement in Palestine (*Al Ahram*, 6–12 November 2003). The Special Unit was also involved in the killing of a prominent magistrate, Ahmad al Khazendar, who had sentenced an MB member to prison for attacking British soldiers (Lia, 1998; Rishwan, interview, 2004). At this time Al Banna felt there was an imbalance in the movement's leadership, and moreover he had no wish to involve his movement in conflict with the Egyptian government. Al Sanadi, however, had enough backing inside the Special Unit to get his own way, unleashing its entire destructive power against the British and the Zionist entity in Palestine. The result of the Unit's violence was the undermining of the MB's political influence; the government now had the justification to launch attacks on the organisation and structure of the movement, banning its branches in Ismailiya and Port Said and arrested a large number of its members (Harris, 1964). The final nail in the MB's coffin came when a vehicle was captured in an ambush set by the security forces, and the Special Unit was exposed. In December 1948 the government of Prime Minister Mahmoud Naqrashi banned the MB, closed down its offices and confiscated its funds and properties. Government justified this move by demonstrating that the MB had stockpiled arms, made bombs and explosives, attacked commercial and security facilities and instigated riots. The Egyptian courts, however, later acquitted the MB of many of these charges, ruling that the Arab League had approved the use of weapons in the Palestinian war.

In the face of the political crisis engulfed the MB, Al Banna decided to change the name of the movement, or to merge it with the Muslim Youth Association. He submitted a proposal to King Farouq to turn the MB into a religious group which would help the monarchy resist communism. Farouq, however, rejected this proposal, and this led to a comprehensive split between the MB and the Palace. It was the first time such a breakdown in communication between the two had occurred since the emergence of the MB; this in turn caused frustration in the ranks of the MB, leading to the assassination of Prime Minister Naqrashi by an MB member, Hassan Taleb (*Shia News*, 22 April 2001; Rishwan, interview, 2004). Taleb claimed that the Prime Minister had been a traitor who had neglected the Palestinian cause, fought against Islam and banned the MB. In retaliation the government arrested and tortured thousands of MB members, forcing the issuing of religious decrees condemning the movement and calling for its dissolution. Al Banna attempted to start a process of reconciliation with the government and the King, but this was short-lived – in February 1949 he was assassinated by the secret police. Al Banna's death was a huge blow for the MB: he had presided over its growth and development since its inception.

The next elected leader of the MB was Hassan Hudaybi, a former court judge and a well-respected member of the Egyptian elite. He adopted a policy based on the *da'wa* ('call to Islam') with 'wisdom and good exhortation' and a less confrontational style than that which had previously characterised the movement (Munson, 2001; Rishwan, interview, 2004; Choubaky, interview, 2004). The shouting of slogans and the emotional language which had characterised MB demonstrations and public rallies were brought to a halt by the new leader; he wanted the movement to adopt a more professional outlook. This policy ultimately clashed with the MB's radical wing, which called for political struggle with the Egyptian state; the internal conflict intensified to the extent that Hudaybi was accused of making peace agreements with King Farouq and of preventing the MB from fighting the British (Lia, 1998; Mitchell, 1969). The discord within the MB was not surprising, as the movement had become accustomed to a certain style of leadership and management, embodied in the charismatic and dynamic personality of Al Banna – anyone succeeding him had a necessarily difficult task to fulfil. While Hudaybi did not possess Al

Banna's personal attributes, nor had the same leadership style, it would be naive to dismiss him as an ineffective and incompetent leader (*Daily Times*, 1 August 2004). He kept the movement intact and functioning in spite of challenges over his leadership, the detention of over 4,000 of its members, and its formal dissolution by the Egyptian government. This was even more impressive as Hudaybi's time as leader coincided with the surfacing of Sayed Qutb and his political discourse, which was diametrically opposed to what Hudaybi believed (Beinin, 2005).

While all this was going on within the MB, the Egyptian regime was decaying, and on 23 July 1952 it was overthrown by a small cadre of military men, known as the 'Free Officers'. This was a significant event for the MB as various members of the movement had strong links with the military and with the Free Officers. The coup provided the MB with an opportunity to influence the political system in accordance with its Islamic vision. They were to be disappointed, however: the Free Officers' vision for Egypt did not coincide with its own, bringing to the surface conflict between the two dominant actors in Egyptian politics at that time.

The Free Officers

Gamal Abdel Nasser, Abdel Monem Abdel Rauf, Khaled Muhiyeddine, Kamaleddine Hussein and Hassan Ibrahim had founded the Free Officers' first cell in July 1949; all five had been members of the MB's Special Unit between 1944 and 1945. Nasser sought the support of all political powers, relying heavily on the support of the MB. The movement's general leadership was convened, and declared its support for the revolution based on reforms founded in Islam. Despite the MB's approval and support for the revolution, difficulties between the factions appeared. In September 1952 Major-General Mohammed Naguib, who had been appointed Commander-in-Chief by the Free Officers, formed a government, but excluded the MB from participation, prompting, the movement to place itself in opposition to the new Egyptian leadership (*Al Ahram*, 27 June–3 July 2002). When a new law regulating the activities of political parties was issued toward the end of 1952, Hudaybi realised that the Free Officers planned to ban political parties, and made every effort to prevent the registration of the MB as a political party – a continuation of his policy of not involving the movement in conflicts. In November 1953 all political parties were banned, with the single exception of the MB; it was then pressured to join the Free Officers' 'Freedom Committee' as a political organisation, but refused to do so, Hudaybi stating that: 'Parties with principles cannot be established through the army and the police' (*Al Ahram*, 27 June–3 July 2002).

By May 1953 tensions between the movement and the new regime began to intensify. Nasser issued a warning to Hudaybi demanding that the MB stop any attempts to recruit members within the army and the police (Mitchell, 1969; Lia, 1998). He also demanded that the MB dissolve the movement's existing branches in the army and security forces, and disband the Special Unit. In a brave move, Hudaybi defied Nasser by rejecting these demands, and began to attack those dissidents within the movement who were defying his leadership by supporting Nasser (Choubaky, interview, 2004; Rishwan, interview, 2004).

As a result of non-compliance by the movement and its stubbornness in refusing to bow down to the demands of the regime, the latter decided, in January 1954 to dissolve the MB. The pretext for this was that the movement maintained contact with the British Embassy in Cairo, that it was opposed to agricultural reform, and that it was attempting to overthrow the regime. The MB reacted by convening a conference in Damascus which condemned the leaders of the 1952 revolution and their decision to ban the movement in Egypt. The MB came to realise that it was virtually impossible to reach an agreement with Nasser, who had begun to perceive the MB as politically dangerous to his rule. The deadlock resulted in frustration inside the ranks of the MB, and this in turn led a member of the movement to attempt Nasser's assassination, while he was delivering a speech in Alexandria on 26 October 1954. This failed, and Nasser cracked down hard on the MB, destroying its structure and organisation (*Al Ahram*, 27 June–3 July 2002; *Al Jazeera*, 22 June 2005).

The Egyptian government detained over 4,000 members of the MB, and began dismantling the movement through a 'People's Tribunal', which imposed harsh sentences on those convicted. The MB called for a popular uprising to overthrow the regime: Hudaybi claimed that an uprising would aim to restore political freedoms and parliamentary life, release prisoners and hand power to civilians. In reaction to this call by the MB, and the consequent risk of political disturbances throughout the country, the People's Tribunal issued death sentences against Hudaybi and many other MB leaders (Choubaky, interview, 2004; Rishwan, interview, 2004). Nasser refused the Syrian government's and the Syrian MB's call not to carry out the executions, and also failed to heed protests from Jordan, Pakistan and Sudan. The power of the MB in Egypt was now effectively eroded, with a large number of its members detained and others executed.

After 1954 the MB stopped its overt activities in Egypt and lost its power as the central leadership of the movement in the Middle East. The leadership consequently passed to Syria, where an 'executive bureau' for the MB in the Middle East was established, led by Issam Attar, the general supervisor of the Syrian MB. During this period of turbulence for the MB, with the Egyptian regime applying heavy pressure, the MB as a whole was able to maintain its structure through the executive bureau (Rishwan, interview, 2004; Choubaky, interview, 2004). The committee included Issam Attar (the MB's leader in Syria), Mohammed Abdel Rahman Khalifah (MB leader in Jordan) Fathi Yakan (head of *al Jammaa al Islamiyya* in Lebanon) and leaders of other MB branches in the Middle East. At that time, the executive bureau formed a commando base in Jordan under the flag of the Palestinian Fatah faction; however internal conflicts arose, and in 1969 the committee collapsed.

By 1974 all detained MB members had been freed. Hudaybi aimed to reconstruct the MB after his own release from prison. He took advantage of the pilgrimage season in Mecca in 1972 and 1973 to hold a meeting in Saudi Arabia of the MB's leaders, in an effort to unify the MB across the Middle East. During the pilgrimage of 1975, the MB, on Hudaybi's initiative, convened a meeting of the 'Founding Committee' (later called the 'International Shura Council') to complete its organisational structure. This was successful in overcoming a prevailing climate of division, and through Hudaybi's initiative the MB was able to overcome another hurdle – a task to which he had become accustomed since taking over the MB leadership. His success on this occasion was momentous, since it revived the ailing organisation, allowing it to operate in a coordinated manner in the Middle East and redirecting leadership back to Egypt. Importantly, this provided a basis for the MB to develop once again into a key political actor in Egypt, able to challenge state power.

Sadat and his search for legitimacy

The fortunes of the MB in the 1970s were assisted by Sadat's pursuit of much-needed legitimacy, in which he realised the importance of religion – even Nasser was aware of this, which had led to the cooptation into the state of religious institutions such as Al Azhar. Religious verdicts from Al Azhar had been used to support domestic control and to promote Nasser's foreign policy objectives. Subordinating Al Azhar to the state also allowed Nasser to balance the influence of the MB, which threatened to challenge the state (Barraclough, 1998). Moreover, Nasser understood that Al Azhar's influence extended well beyond the borders of Egypt, and that government control over the most respected and influential institution of Islamic scholarship would be an important tool in furthering Egypt's leadership of Arab and Islamic nations. As Islam was the dominant religion in Egypt and the wider Middle East, it was politically expedient and shrewd of Nasser to use Islam to develop legitimacy in order to persist in power. This was also true of Sadat, in particular given the rise of Islamic consciousness in Egyptian society in the aftermath of the 1967 Arab defeat at the hands of Israel. In the 1970s Sadat initiated a debate in his semi-official press through Al Azhar about what was described as the 'Islamic economy' and its compatibility with capitalist ethos and values (Moustafa, 2000). In addition, Islam was used by Sadat to project in public a personal image of religious piety. Sadat promoted himself as the 'believing president', and was constantly seen at prayer. The 1971 constitution stipulated that: 'Islam is the religion of the state; Arabic is the official language; and the principles of the Islamic *Shariah* are a principal source of legislation'. Even more significant than the inclusion of this article in the constitution was the Egyptian state's relationship with the MB. The latter had gone underground in response to its outlawing by Nasser and to the campaign of persecution that followed, which had resulted in thousands of MB members being jailed and a similar number fleeing to surrounding Arab countries to escape the persecution. Sadat's perception of the MB was somewhat different to that of Nasser. He realised the importance of the MB in boosting the state's Islamic image and in acting as a counterweight to the leftist opposition (Kodmani, 2005). As a result, in the early 1970s Sadat developed a policy of accommodating the MB in society. The government released detained members of the MB and allowed exiled members to return to Egypt, for example Yusuf Al Qaradawi, Ahmad al Asaf and Salim Nijm (Al-Awadi, 2004). The MB was also allowed to reclaim its headquarters in Cairo, reconvene its regular meetings inside the mosques, and continue its activities on university campuses and its recruitment of new members (Kodmani, 2005). Thus the MB was allowed to re-enter Egyptian society, which began a new phase in the life of the movement. This in turn resulted in the MB undergoing changes to its shape and character, leading to its participation in parliament and professional syndicates and to the forming of party alliances – thus allowing it to construct a challenge to state power in the 1990s, at a time of economic reform.

Conclusion

This chapter has explored the evolution of the MB, through an examination of its growth and development from 1928 to the 1970s, allowing it to become a key political actor in Egypt. However, from the 1970s onwards the political weight of the MB was extended through the extensive changes it underwent in its shape and character. These changes led to a transition from the spiritual to the political, through its involvement in various institutions, and thus to construct enough power to challenge the Egyptian government at a time of economic reform and socio-economic crisis in the 1990s.

5

FROM PIETY TO POLITICS: CHANGING DISCOURSE, ALLIANCES AND ACTIVISM

This chapter continues to analyse the changing shape and character of the MB as it moved from spiritual piety to political activism, examining the introduction of the MB into formal politics in the 1980s through its participation in parliamentary elections. This participation represented a key change in the character of the MB, allowing it to construct enough political weight to challenge Egyptian state power at a time of socio-economic crisis in the 1990s.

Changing political discourse: from Hassan Al Banna to Sayed Qutb

During the 1930s the MB was viewed as a social movement, with its activities predominantly devoted to the moral and spiritual reformation of society (Mitchell, 1969; Abd al Monein and Wenner, 1982). However, with the movement's transition to politics in the late 1930s, led by Al Banna, it set forth more specific political and executive goals for governance. The first was to put an end to the party system and point the political community in a single direction (Hassan, 2005). According to some theological interpretations of Islamic texts, a system of political parties is to be viewed as sinister, a cause of evil and discord in society, allowing entities to emerge that threaten the Islamic fabric of society. This divides the *umma* (Muslim community) and places groups at odds with one another, further causing a form of sectarianism rather than cohesion (Hassan, 2005). Another objective declared by Al Banna was to strengthen ties between Islamic circles in other countries, especially over the entire Arab region, thus reviving the idea of an Islamic caliphate. Al Banna also stressed the need for Muslims to show concern for each other's suffering, through highlighting the concept of belonging to the *umma*. Al Banna showed in practice what this meant in his reaction to the Palestinian crisis in the 1930s and 1940s (Hassan, 2005). He instructed the movement to address the Palestinian crisis through the distribution of leaflets, sermons in the mosque and the holding of demonstrations to rally the Egyptian people – in the midst of Al Banna's social and economic thought there was an expression of politics. However, Al Banna's political discourse was challenged during the 1950s and 1960s, following the rise of Sayed Qutb, and the development of the latter's own discourse.

During his early career Sayed Qutb devoted himself to literature as an author and critic, writing novels such as *Ashwak* ('Thorns') and even elevating Egyptian novelist Naguib Mahfouz from obscurity. After his graduation from Dar al Ulum in 1933, Qutb began a teaching career, eventually becoming involved in Egypt's Ministry of Education (Khatab, 2006; Shepard, 1996), which sent him to the US, to research Western methods of teaching. He spent two years there, from 1948 to 1950, studying at Wilson's Teachers' College on the east coast before moving west and earning an MA in Education at the University of Northern Colorado (Abdel Malek, 2000: 10). In 'The America I Have Seen', a personal account of Qutb's experiences in the US, he applauds the economic and scientific progress and the achievements of the US, but at the same time expresses his dismay at the primitive level of sense, feeling and behaviour among the people (Qutb, 2000:

11). By this Qutb was alluding to values such as freedom, indi-
vidualism and materialism, which formed the functional basis of
American society (Shepard, 1996; Haddad, 1983; Mousalli, 1992;
Khan, 1998). He believed that these values had led to the social
problems America was facing, such as high levels of consumerism,
sexual discrimination and promiscuity (Henzel, 2005; *Al Ahram*,
11–17 March 1999). As a result Qutb believed that America was
in a state of *jahiliyya* ('ignorance') (Qutb, 2002; Shepard, 1996;
Rahnema, 1994; McGregor, 2003; *Al Ahram*, 9–15 December
1999). Qutb, being a devout Muslim, believed that the prophet
Muhammad was sent as a messenger of God's guidance, and that
the Qur'an is His final message for man to live life in obedience to
Him, bringing happiness and harmony. For Qutb, therefore, those
who ignore it are guilty of *jahiliyya*. Qutb believed that throughout
human history men have disobeyed God; as a result God has sent
man help whenever he falls into *jahiliyya*:

> When this state of affairs is reached (*jahiliyya*), God sends
> a messenger to human beings explaining to them the very
> same truth they had had before sinking into *jahiliyya*. Some
> of them write their own destruction, while others are able
> to spare themselves by returning to the truth of the faith.
> These are the ones ... who listen to their messenger as he
> says to them: My people worship God alone: you have no
> deity other than Him (Qur'an 7, trans. Abdel Haleem, p.
> 59).

Therefore, *jahiliyya* results whenever man ignores the divine
commands given by God's messengers. Qutb used Surah 7 in
the Qur'an as an extensive example of how truth (Islam) and
falsity (*jahiliyya)* have battled throughout human history. He
believed that this Surah 'portrays how those in the procession
of faith try to rescue man every time he strays far away from
the right path' (Qutb, 2002: 122). As with American society, to

Qutb the Nasserist regime had strayed far from the right path, which led him to reject its ideology, values and practices, classifying them as *jahiliyya* – in contradicting the Islamic message (Khatab, 1996; 2006; Qutb, 1991). Qutb believed that Al Azhar had also strayed from the right path by being pressed into the service of Nasserism (Choubaky, interview, 2004). As a result, Rishwan, interview, 2004); as a result, Egyptian society had to be brought back to the straight path, and the first necessity was the removal of Nasser's regime, to cleanse the country of his blend of socialism and nationalism. This would also, according to Qutb, allow Al Azhar to break the shackles of the regime and to act in the service of Islam. Qutb, through his work *Ma'alim fi al-Tariq* ('Signposts' or 'Milestones'), which centred on key concepts such as *jahiliyya*, *haq* ('truth') vs. *batil* ('falsity'), *kufar* ('non-belief') and *al-'adala al-ijtima'iyya* ('social justice'), created considerable zeal in the ranks of the MB. He also gave its members hope that they would be the vanguard of a successful challenge to the dominant ideology of Nasserism, and would lay the foundations for a truly Islamic community in Egypt. Shukri Mustafa led those who adopted Qutb's view that Egypt was in a state of unbelief, and that the brotherhood should prepare for an active struggle to establish a proper Islamic state. After his release from prison, Mustafa established *Jama'at al-Muslimin* ('Society of Muslims'), better known as the *Takfir wa al-Hijra* group – meaning roughly to retreat from a society of unbelief (Kepel, 2002; Kramer, 1996; Fuller, 2003). According to Daniel Benjamin and Steven Simon:

> In a century in which some of the most important writing came out of prisons, Qutb, for better or for worse, is the Islamic world's answer to Solzhenitsyn, Sartre, and Havel, and he easily ranks with all of them in influence. It was Sayyid Qutb who fused together the core elements of modern Islamism ... Qutb concluded that the unity of

> God and His sovereignty meant that human rule – govern-
> ment legislates its own behavior – is illegitimate – Muslims
> must answer to God alone. (2002: 62)

The old-guard leadership of the MB rejected the concepts expressed in *Ma'alim fi al-Tariq* and affirmed the movement's historic position that through preaching (*da'wa*) Muslims could be brought to a higher state of commitment and practice. In 1969 the society's second General Guide, Hasan al Hudaybi, wrote a strong reply to Qutb: *Du'a, La Quda* ('Preachers, Not Judges'). Hudaybi repudiated the violence employed by the Brothers' Rovers, the MB's Special Unit in 1947–49 and 1954. Umar al Tilemensani, who became General Guide in 1973, shared the views of the old-guard leadership (Choubaky, interview, 2004; *Al Ahram*, 11–17 March 1999). However, unlike them, Al Tilemensani was prag-matic, a visionary, who sought to lead the MB to new ground by shifting it from its traditional focus on spiritual piety towards political activism. This would be indicative of the growing changes in the shape and character of the MB, which were stepped up in the 1980s and 1990s.

Umar Al Tilemensani and changes in the Muslim Brotherhood

In the 1970s the MB experienced a new lease of life, as thousands of its members were released from prison, exiled members were allowed back into Egypt and the movement was allowed to recom-mence its activities. As a result of this the movement began actively to pursue two simultaneous objectives (Al-Awadi, 2004). The first was to secure legal status for the MB from the Egyptian govern-ment, which it had lost in 1954. The second was to rebuild the organisation, which had been destroyed by Nasser (Choubaky, interview, 2004; Madi, interview, 2004). The first objective would be an arduous task, but an important one if the MB was to have a secure future in Egypt.

To acquire legal status for the MB, Tilemensani filed a court case in October 1977 against Nasser's 1954 decision to disband the organisation (Baker, 1990). Tilemensani's argument was based on the premise that the Revolutionary Council had lacked any real legislative or constitutional rights; consequently the decision of the Nasserist regime to outlaw the MB was invalid. The decision to contest the outlawing of the MB was strengthened by Sadat's political reforms, such as the political party law of 1976 (Al-Awadi, 2004). The transition from a one-party to a multi-party system gave the MB hope that its illegal status would soon be overturned. However, this hope was short-lived: Tilemensani's case was not settled by the court. The MB quickly realised that even Sadat's judicial system, however independent it appeared to be on the surface, was in reality part of the state apparatus and without any real independent decision-making powers. The long delay in the court's verdict on the future of the MB led to growing levels of anger and frustration in the movement's ranks. Given this delay, Tilemensani took the view that a decision might never emerge, or the ban might thus not be overturned (Al-Awadi, 2004). Also, Tilemensani was aware that the Egyptian government's rather tolerant policy towards the movement could change, reverting to a policy of coercion. Thus, having examined all possible scenarios, none of which were positive, Tilemensani realised that the movement had to change in order to force the overturning of the ban and to avoid possible coercion from the government. He believed the change needed was a shift in the work of the movement, from its traditional focus on spiritual piety to political activism. This transition indicated a change in the shape and character of the movement, allowing the MB to become once again a key political actor in Egypt, able to challenge the state in the 1990s at a time of the heightened socio-economic crisis (Choubaky, interview, 2004; Rishwan, interview, 2004; Madi, interview, 2004).

However, the launching of Tilemensani's new policy was not straightforward: he faced opposition from the old-guard leadership in the movement, who were more conservative in their thinking and approach, formed by the harsh experience of the MB's repression under Nasser. For example, Mohammed Akef, who was much later to become *Murshid* (Leader) of the group, was already a member when Al Banna was assassinated in 1949. He was sentenced to death after the failed 1954 assassination attempt of Nasser, and remained in prison until 1974. He and others of his generation, who formed the core of the old guard, were generally more zealous and conservative, and were committed primarily to long-term spiritual work and to preserving the movement's unity (Altman, 2006). The old guard was and continues to be deeply suspicious of other groups and unforgiving toward former political rivals such as the Nasserists, Arab nationalists and Marxists, due to ideological differences and bitter past confrontations. They followed the religious teachings of Al Banna, who, although later in his life himself involved in politics, remained a political sceptic, especially with respect to party politics in Egypt: he saw party politics as representing a key source of conflict and division in society (Mitchell, 1969). This perception was shaped by his stay in Cairo between 1923 and 1927, when party politics was inundated by corruption, conflict and rivalry. As a result, politics had done much more harm than good to society, and there was therefore a need to distance the movement from party politics to prevent it from falling into the vicious trap of corruption, conflict and rivalry. Instead Al Banna stressed the need to give advice to the Egyptian monarchy and government, in order to allow the MB to discharge its religious duty to the political order, without getting dragged into the dirty life of party politics. Al Banna's political thinking shaped the views of the old-guard leadership, who as a result were uncomfortable with a transition of the MB from the spiritual to the political (Lia, 1998). Given that the old guard still played a key role in the MB's decision-making, being institutionalised within its chain of command, Tilemensani knew he would have a difficult time in convincing this faction to support the change in the movement's character, from its traditional piety to political activism. As Tilemensani saw this change as being vital for the movement's future, he was willing to challenge the dominance of the old-guard leadership to present his vision and to drive forward the changes he believed to be necessary.

This process of change was evident when Tilemensani began to speak about the prospect of the MB participating in Sadat's parliament (Al-Awadi, 2004). There was strong opposition from the old guard, who saw this move as being at odds with the MB's orthodox role of spiritual guidance, but Tilemensani was unconcerned by this – in fact he welcomed it as contributing to internal discussion on the changing shape and character of the MB. He continued to stress the transition of the MB from the spiritual to the political, to work towards the overturning of the ban on the MB, and to avoid possible oppression by the government. Despite internal clashes within the movement, Tilemensani hoped that Sadat would agree to admit it into parliament, as representative of an independent socio-economic and political trend in Egyptian society. His hope can be seen as a compromise with the old guard, as Tilemensani did not demand that the movement be admitted into parliament on a party-political platform (Al-Awadi, 2004; Rishwan, interview, 2004). However, Sadat was seriously concerned that the MB might evolve into an effective political opposition to his government, and so was disinclined to allow the movement this independent representation in parliament. Instead, Sadat gave the MB the option of participating in parliament through a coalition with any of the three existing political parties which had emerged after the dissolution of the Arab Socialist Union (ASU) in 1976. However, Tilemensani refused Sadat's offer, perceiving that any form of coalition with the secular political opposition would damage the MB's public image as an Islamic actor in Egyptian society, and result in major opposition from the old guard, who viewed the secular parties with disdain (Choubaky, interview, 2004; Madi, interview, 2004). However, this setback did not deter Tilemensani, as he was convinced that the state would in the end be forced to accept the MB if it continued in its drive to move from spiritual to political activity. Tilemensani wanted to see more changes in the movement, and these were facilitated by the rise of a new generation of members in the late 1970s and early 1980s, who introduced a new culture of politics into the MB. This new generation would drive the process of change and the contestation of political power, resulting in the movement developing into a key political force by the time of economic reform in the 1990s.

The rise of the new generation in the Muslim Brotherhood

Since the time of Al Banna the MB's old-guard leadership had focused on maintaining its own power, neglected the need to educate new leaders and worked to conserve the MB unchanged (*Al Jazeera*, 4 December 2002). This focus by the old guard meant that they were seen to care more about internal structure, to maintain their own position and power, than about a process of change that would allow the MB to construct a challenge to state power (Altman, 2006). However, after decades of domination within the MB this old guard was eventually challenged by the emergence of a new generation. This latter differed from the old guard on a number of key issues: how internal decisions should be made; how a leader should be elected; the state; the West; and the function of the movement. The new generation, with its blend of Islamic politics and pragmatism, facilitated the changing shape of the movement.

The new generation came on the scene during the late 1970s and early 1980s (Choubaky, 2004). Their experience was different from the old guard's, which of course influenced their thinking and their approach to the movement – for example they had not experienced Nasser's oppression in the 1950s and 1960s, but had become familiar with limited political openness and with participation in student politics through the *Jama'at Islamiyya* ('Islamic student movement') in the 1970s (Olav Utvik, 2005; Baker, 2003; Brown et al, 2006). Through student politics, which entailed daily interaction with students of different ideologies, rapprochement with different student groups and standing for student-union elections, the new guard acquired a greater taste for politics. This can be deduced from the fact that the new generation attached greater importance to politics than to spiritual matters: they saw Egypt, rather than the Muslim world, as the MB's real frame of reference, and were interested in building alliances with secular political organisations as a way of dealing with pressing socio-economic issues. The new generation included Essam El Eryian, assistant secretary-general of the Doctors' Syndicate, Ibrahim El-Zafrani, secretary-general of the same syndicate's Alexandria chapter, Mohamed Habib, an Asiut University professor, and Abdel Moneim Abul Futuh from the Guidance Bureau Council (Choubaky, interview, 2004; Rishwan, interview, 2004). When these individuals joined the MB, they were followed by a large section of the rank-and-file members of the Islamic student movement, which had been led in the 1970s by new guard activists such as El Eyrian, Abul Ella Madi and Abul Futuh (Olav Utvik, 2005). As a result the new generation had a loyal support base which supported the changes it was pushing for, leading to inevitable clashes with the old-guard leadership. These clashes were already evident in the 1980s, and escalated during the 1990s, as the pragmatic newcomers sped up the process of change in the MB.

In the mid-1990s the new generation's drive to change the shape and character of the MB led to the formation of a party manifesto for *Hizb al Wasat* (the Centre Party) (Stacher, 2001; 2002; Olav Utvik, 2005; Rumaihi, 1997) – a clear attempt to form a legal arm through which it could operate in society. However, the committee of political parties rejected *Hizb al Wasat*'s application for legal status, and this caused problems in the ranks of the MB over how to proceed next. New generation members such as Abul Ella Madi and Salah Abdel Karim wanted to continue the political-party initiative to bring about further change in the nature of the MB (Madi, interview, 2004; Stacher, 2001; Olav Utvik, 2005). They sought to adapt the *Hizb al Wasat* manifesto to make it more palatable to the government. However, the old guard saw no benefit in this: they believed it would be rejected by the Egyptian government regardless of the number of amendments (Madi, interview, 2004). As a result of this deadlock and disagreement, Madi, Abdel Karim and other seasoned new-generation members left the movement in order to proceed with the *al Wasat* group. This group represented certain elements of the new MB generation which had become tired of the old guard's dogmatic approach and decided to branch out on their own and try their luck in Egyptian politics (Stacher, 2002). For example, in a January 1995 editorial in the magazine of the Engineers' Union, editor Salah Abdel Karim, later a central member of the *al Wasat* group, indirectly criticised the domination of the old guard and pointed out the necessity for a proper division of work among the two generations, a division whereby the movement's elders should restrict themselves to the role of advisors (Olav Utvik, 2005). Much more explicit criticism was expressed in a speech, *al-infitah al-nafsi wa al-'amal al-'am* ('psychological openness and public work'), given at an internal meeting for MB members active in the unions. As the title suggests, the old guard was criticised for being too narrow-minded and inward-looking when there was a need for openness toward social and political forces other than the MB itself (Olav Utvik, 2005; Rumaihi, 1997).

The principal founders of *Hizb al Wasat*, Abul Ella Madi and Salah Abdel Karim, pursued a liberal approach, claiming the party was 'civilisational', one for all Egyptians irrespective of race, religion or ethnicity (Madi, interview, 2004; Choubaky, interview, 2004). Abul Ella Madi and Abdel Karim have argued that *Hizb al Wasat* has a clear position on key issues such as human rights, Copts, democracy and the role of women (Olav Utvik, 2005; Stacher, 2001; 2002). To some the party could be viewed as on the left of the political spectrum, as it promotes social work and trade unionism and is critical of economic policies such as privatisation and the reduction of state subsidies (Hamzawy, interview, 2004). The country's intellectual elite is supportive of Abul Ella Madi and Abdel Karim: they see *Hizb al Wasat* as a counterweight to the solely religious trend represented in the MB (Madi, interview, 2004). This elite was supportive of the new generation in the movement, and remains suspicious of the old-guard leadership, which continues to hold a dominant position. Diaa Rishwan, an expert on political Islam at the Al-Ahram Center for Political and Strategic Studies, predicted two potential scenarios, if the Egyptian government had decided to allow *Hizb al Wasat* to function in society (Rishwan, Interview, 2004):

- waves of MB members, especially the new generation, defect to *Hizb al Wasat*, to gain control and to change it in conformity with their own politics and their own approach to Islam;
- the MB refuses all cooperation with *Hizb al Wasat*, and attacks it; as a result the party finds it difficult to make any impact on Egyptian society.

It is clear that the case of *Hizb al Wasat* highlighted a clear cultural clash between the old-guard leasership and the new generation. To the former, this clash indicated the need to keep the latter content, in order to avoid endangering their own position of power within the movement. This was a key factor behind the old guard's appointment of Mohammed Akef as the new General Guide in 2004. Although Akef was one of their number, his appointment was indicative of the need to recognise the growing role of the new generation inside the movement, since Akef was willing to listen to and take into consideration the views presented by new-generation members such as Abul Futuh and El Eyrian. However, Akef, leader until 2010, was seen by the old-guard leadership as able to check and control the rise of the new generation, and thus to secure their own position in the MB. The old guard will continue to play a key role in the movement, but there is no doubt that the new generation have achieved a certain prominence, as can be seen in the fact that they have dominated the public face of the MB through their participation over the past 25 years in the People's Assembly, professional syndicates and the media. It was in fact their participation in the 1984 parliamentary elections which started the process of their rise to prominence and their drive to bring change to the MB. This provided the basis for the movement to become a key political actor by the time of the economic reforms in the 1990s.

The new generation in the MB: politics and party alliances

President Hosni Mubarak faced his first parliamentary elections in 1984. To ensure a comfortable two-thirds majority for the NDP, the electoral law was changed. The new law confined political activism to legal political parties, thus excluding independent candidates from standing (Hassan, 2005; Ibrahim, 1988). Also, according to this electoral law all participating political parties needed to reach a threshold of 8 per cent of the votes to acquire seats inside the People's Assembly. This threshold was extremely high, reducing the chances of a political party acquiring parliamentary seats (Tripp and Owen, 1991; Wickham, 2002; Abdel Kotob, 1995), and to reach it was a mammoth task, given the autocratic control which the government exercised over Egyptian society, through the use of its coercive arm and the state of emergency. The electoral law led the new MB generation, and Tilemensani, to consider changing the MB's character to allow participation in the 1984 elections: since there was no possibility of the movement overturning the ban, the only way for it to compete in the elections was by constructing an alliance with the secular opposition (Al-Awadi, 2004). Apart from competing in the elections, Tilemensani and the new generation believed that such an alliance would benefit the movement in other ways (Choubaky, interview, 2004; Hamzawy, interview, 2004): it would allow the MB to develop a public platform – through which it could demonstrate its shift from religion to politics – and to gain essential political experience, which it lacked in comparison to the secular opposition. This political experience and exposure would be important in allowing the new generation to change the shape and character of the MB, in turn allowing the movement to challenge the power and authority of the Egyptian government (Choubaky, interview, 2004; Rishwan, interview, 2004).

After long deliberation the MB decided to build a political alliance with *al Wafd* party. This was a daring move, given the stark ideological differences and historical confrontation between the MB and *al Wafd*. The new generation were conscious of the criticism which would emanate from the old-guard leadership, whose members had from the beginning been uncomfortable with the changing nature of the MB (Choubaky, interview, 2004). However, this was something the new generation were willing to risk to allow the MB to enter the parliamentary elections – a major step in the transition of the movement from religion to politics. In the event, the gamble paid off – the political alliance between the MB and *al Wafd* in the 1984 parliamentary elections turned out a success, securing 58 seats in the People's Assembly, with eight of these assigned to the MB (Maye, 2004; Wickham, 2002; Langhor, 2001). The conduct of the movement's representatives in parliament surprised many from the political opposition – where they were expected to deal in overt religious polemics and slogans, their behaviour came to be viewed as very competent and professional, their opinions articulated without recourse to the religious rhetoric the secular opposition had feared. Also, the MB's presence in parliament showed the possible challenge it could pose to the government; but the latter failed to act – Mubarak still sought legitimacy. This failure eventually backfired on the government: the MB underwent further changes, which allowed it, in the 1990s, to construct a key political role for itself and to mount its challenge to the government.

The MB's success in the 1984 parliamentary elections, and the new generation's demonstrable political competence, indicated to them and to Tilemensani that the movement had the capacity to survive in the political sytem and to challenge the government. However, they believed that further changes were still necessary for this challenge to be mounted. Tilemensani began to contemplate the creation of an independent political party to act as legal cover for the MB. In the minds of the old-guard leadership, to accept such a notion was not easy, but much less difficult than a transformation of the *tanzim* ('movement') into a political force, which had been the main topic of discussions during the late 1970s (Madi, interview, 2004; Choubaky, interview, 2004). The new proposal thus enabled a compromise to be reached, whereby the *tanzim* could effectively co-exist with its legal political cover. The plan was that the movement would continue working on the spiritual plane, while the independent political party would make political inroads, speeding up the process of change in the character of the movement led by the new generation (Madi, interview, 2004). Despite this apparent compromise there was a need to convince the old guard that a political arm would not endanger its position and power in the MB. In a statement Tilemensani distinguished between the roles of the *tanzim* and the MB's putative political organ:

> The *Ikhwan* is an international organisation and its concerns encompass the entire world and continents. This is different from political parties, which have domestic concerns. The [ruling] democratic party does not have branches in

England or America, while the *Ikhwan* has branches all over the world. (Al-Awadi, 2004: 83)

Tilemensani dealt not only with the concerns of the old-guard leadership by emphasising the importance of the *tanzim*, but also with the growing demands of the new generation by directing the preparation of a party manifesto to act as a platform for the MB's potential political arm. In reply to Tilemensani's initiative two separate manifesto drafts were prepared by members, led by the new generation. One draft would have been for *Hizb al Islam al Misri* ('Egyptian Reform Party') and the second for *Hizb al Shura* ('Consultation Party') (Al-Awadi, 2004; Choubaky, interview, 2004; Madi, interview, 2004). In the event, neither was submitted to the government, for fear of outright rejection: the belief among the new leadership was that the movement had to go further before the Egyptian government would allow it to create a political arm (Al-Awadi, 2004).

The 1987 parliamentary elections provided the new generation with another opportunity to demonstrate further the changing character of the MB. In these elections the movement formed another political alliance, but this time with *al Amal* party and *Hizb al Ahrar* ('Liberal Party'). This was further evidence of the MB's changing character, as it was willing to cross more ideological barriers in adding to its growing political weight in Egytian politics (*Al Ahram*, 26 October–1 November 1995). Despite sharply divergent ideologies and political programmes, the two opposition parties united with the MB to support programmes of democratic reforms which aimed to breaking the NDP's electoral stranglehold. This time the MB gained 36 seats, a massive increase from the eight it had won in 1984. With this impressive showing it had created a concerted political opposition inside the People's Assembly, posing a real challenge to the dominance of the NDP inside the legislative body. Furthermore, given that the movement's 36 members represented the new generation leadership, they were

young, educated, professional, politically aware and responsive to
the needs of the constituents they represented, addressing broad
issues such as the government's policies on health and education.
They were also critical of the government's attitude to economic
problems such as growing unemployment, corruption, inflation,
debt and massive consumption (Al-Awadi, 2004). In this political
outlook, the new MB members in the People's Assembly could
not be distinguished from the rest of the (secular) opposition in
their thinking and conduct, marking a clear shift away from religion and towards politics (Hamzawy, interview, 2004; Choubaky,
interview, 2004).

The 1990 parliamentary election was boycotted by the MB,
along with the secular opposition (except *al Tagammu* party). The
decision to take this step was attributable to a number of reasons,
such as corruption and the continuation of the state of emergency
(Maye, 2004). However, the decision was not accepted by all in
the movement, in particular the new-generation leadership (Maye,
2004) – they would have preferred to take the opportunity of
further strengthening the MB's political position and to win over
sceptics by demonstrating further internal changes. There was thus
frustration among some members. However, the boycott did not
indicate an end to changes within the movement, nor did it indicate
a victory for the old guard – the MB did participate in the People's
Assembly elections four years later. There was much enthusiasm
surrounding the 1995 elections, as they witnessed an unprecedented rise in the number of independent candidates standing
for election. Official estimates indicated that more than 4,000
candidates contested the Assembly's 444 seats; 439 were from the
NDP, 181 from *al Wafd* party, 107 from *al Amal* party, and 170
from the MB, while the rest either belonged to smaller parties or
were independents (*Al Ahram*, 2–8 November 1995). However,
this enthusiasm ended when the elections became marred by an
unprecedented level of violence and intimidation on the part of
the security forces, including coercive interference to prevent the

political opposition, and the MB in particular, from succeeding at the polls (Kienle, Spring 1998). Hundreds of political activists and voters were harassed by the police and the security forces; some 60 people were killed and as many as 878 severely injured in violent disturbances outside voting stations (Maye, 2004; *Al Ahram*, 14–20 December 1995).

The government provided a number of justifications for this coercive response by the police and security forces during the elections (Campagna, 1996). The electorate was portrayed as the culprits, instigators of violence, with the police and security forces merely responding to the ensuing crisis. However, despite the government's attempts to justify its conduct, there is no doubt that the key reason for the brutality was the MB's decision to put forward 170 candidates in the elections (Brownlee, 2002; Al-Awadi, 2004). The government had realised that if the MB was allowed to participate in a free and fair election, an overwhelming proportion of the movement's candidates would win seats in the Assembly. This prospect, of an MB bloc in parliament, was a fearful one for the government. For example, if 140 out of the 170 MB candidates had gained seats, this would have posed a direct challenge to the NDP domination of the Assembly. A counter-hegemonic bloc shaped by the MB would have confronted the government with a host of dilemmas, with the situation made even more difficult as the bloc would be led by new-generation members skilled in politics and aware of the social and economic realities in Egypt. In addition, the Assembly was due in 1995 to nominate Mubarak for a fourth term as President, and a powerful presence of the movement would obstruct the nomination process (Al-Awadi, 2004; Brownlee, 2002). Thus it was fear of a strong MB presence in the Assembly, at a time of socio-economic crisis, that determined the government's political strategy, leading the Interior Ministry to interfere excessively in the 1995 elections. The impact of this interference can be seen in the outcome of the elections: out of 170 MB candidates only one candidate succeeded in gaining a seat (Al-Awadi,

2004). However, even that single representative, Essam El Eyrian, had only a short stay in the Assembly: he was immediately accused of belonging to an outlawed religious movement, and his membership of the Assembly was revoked (Maye, 2004; Choubaky, interview, 2004). The government's policy of accommodation towards the MB witnessed during the 1980s had ended, with the state adopting a coercive and confrontational policy. Essentially this was because by the 1990s the movement had become a different entity from that of the 1980s: it had built its *tanzim*, increased its membership, and shifted further away from the spiritual and toward the political. All this had allowed the movement to pose a political challenge to the government, at a time, moreover, of socio-economic crisis.

The government's coercive policy towards the MB in the 1995 elections raised concerns in the old guard, who believed that the government was genuinely autocratic and would not contemplate any challenge to its authority, that there was therefore only a minimal possibility of the MB evolving into a political power, and that changes in the movement's shape and character were doing it more harm than good (Madi, interview, 2004; Rishwan, interview, 2004). They began to emphasise the need for the MB to revert to its traditional spiritual work of building society according to religious virtues and principles, rather than changing the character of the movement to challenge the Egyptian government. The old guard began to reassert their influence over the MB, but the new generation were not demotivated by the government's attitude and continued to push for the movement to become more political. Further politicisation excited them, fully conscious as they were that the government was vulnerable at this time of socio-economic crisis.

As a result the new generation participated in the 2000 parliamentary election, and their performance was much better than in 1995 when the electoral process was marred by violence and an excessive security clamp-down. The movement acquired 17 seats in the People's Assembly, which made it the largest opposition force in parliament. The result took everybody by surprise, including its own members (Choubaky, interview, 2004), and was not predicted by the government, which believed that the MB was too weak after the 1995 clamp-down. This morale-boosting victory against the autocratic state indicated the resilient nature of the MB, in particular of its new generation, and also that reprisals by the government were not going to deter them from working towards the movement's transition from spiritual piety to political activism.

Thus the new generation, by participating in parliamentary elections from 1984 onwards, was able to change the shape and character of the MB, allowing it to challenge the government. This challenge was a source of concern for the government in the 1990s. The situation was complicated by a socio-economic crisis resulting from economic reform, and also by the participation of the new MB generation in professional syndicates. This new generation was making use of all possible political space available to it in Egyptian society to challenge the hegemony of the government – a challenge which was made even more enticing by the socio-economic crisis.

Conclusion

This chapter has focused on the transition of the MB from spiritual piety to political activism, examining the movement's new generation of leaders and their contribution to its changing shape and character that resulted in its entering parliamentary politics and forming party alliances. This allowed it to become a more viable source of political opposition and to challenge the government in the 1990s, at a time of socio-economic crisis. As a result of this opposition and challenge, the government used its coercive apparatus to contain and weaken the MB. A clear example of this was the violence which surrounded the 1995 and 2000 parliamentary elections, and the large-scale detention of the movement's members from 1995 to 2000. A problem for the government, however, was the MB's ability to challenge its hegemony through alternative institutions in civil society, such as professional syndicates. These syndicates would become central to the challenge which the movement mounted during the time of economic reform and of the resultant socio-economic crisis. It is therefore important to explore the role of the MB in civil society to determine how it constructed its challenge through these syndicates.

6

THE ART OF POLITICS: THE NEW GENERATION AND THE SYNDICATES

This chapter explores the MB's involvement in professional syndicates in Egypt and how the movement's new generation of leaders used these institutions to build a power base from which to challenge the position of the state, at a time of socio-economic crisis. The entry of the MB into professional syndicates during the 1980s allowed it to develop a political platform to build support and mobilise syndicate members to oppose and confront the government.

The Egyptian state and professional syndicates

There are approximately 24 professional syndicates in Egypt, with a total of 3.5 million members (Fahmy, 1998; 2002). The objective of these syndicates is to protect the interests of their members, including salaries, pensions, conditions of work and the regulation of entry into the profession concerned. According to Qandil, an expert on MB involvement in syndicates, 'the syndicates also provide an avenue within which less influential and less prestigious subgroups of various professions may attempt to further their socioeconomic and political causes' (interview, 2004). For example, doctors, teachers and lawyers employed by the Egyptian state have all attempted in the past to increase their economic status and rewards through syndicate activities (Wickham, 2002).

Besides providing social settings through which personal contacts and relations can be established, syndicates have also performed an important political role and function. They have pressed the government for concessions which go beyond the traditional syndicate remit of professional activities. The physicians' syndicate successfully resisted the introduction of fully socialised medicine in the early 1960s, and the journalists' syndicate has since the 1950s been the most vocal advocate of the relaxing of media censorship in Egypt (Choubaky, interview, 2004). The lawyers' syndicate, during its heyday in the 1970s, challenged the state on domestic and foreign-policy issues, such as economic liberalisation, privatisation and the Camp David Peace Accords (*Al Ahram*, 14–20 July 2005). Ahmed El-Khawaga, a Nasserist, pursued highly publicised and often ferocious battles with the authorities in the 1970s through the lawyers' syndicate, challenging the government on economic and political issues (*Al Ahram*, 14–20 July 2005). In addition, other syndicates have sponsored debates and published commentaries in their magazines with political overtones, such as on land ownership (agricultural engineers' syndicate), the SUMED (Suez-Mediterranean) pipeline (engineers' syndicate) and educational curricula (teachers' syndicate) (*Al-Ahram*, 14–20 July 2005; Choubaky, Interview, 2004).

The real political significance of the syndicates in Egypt lies in their role as vehicles for mobilising the support of the professional class (Choubaky, interview, 2004). According to Amr Choubaky, a leading commentator on the MB, 'the journalists, doctors, engineers, lawyers and other professionals represent Egypt's articulate sector and if mobilised could represent a real challenge to the Egyptian state's power' (interview, 2004). As a result the syndicates, since 1952, were an arena of concern and thus of intervention on the part of the state (Bianchi, 1989: 106). The government dissolved syndicate boards, co-opted their chairmen, infiltrated syndicates through the use of its security apparatus, and relied upon the compliance of state employees within syndicates (Fahmy, 2002). Nasser and Sadat both kept a close eye on the syndicates in order to keep the professional class under their control and preempt any challenges to their rule. Both also resorted to a major crackdown on syndicates when they felt threatened by them. Between 1964 and 1967, for example, Nasser launched a massive campaign to weaken and discredit them (*Al Ahram*, 14–20 July 2005; Qandil, interview, 2004), to deal with the perceived political danger of syndicates, and to present the ASU as the principal organisation for popular mobilisation in Egypt. Sadat also turned against the syndicates, in particular the lawyers' syndicate after it criticised the peace agreement with Israel (Choubaky, interview, 2004; Hamzawy, interview, 2004), which led to the development of conflict and struggle between the Egyptian state and the lawyers' syndicate.

However, the fortunes of syndicates in Egypt changed after the assassination of Sadat, when Hosni Mubarak came to power in 1981. Mubarak began a process of limited political liberalisation, wherein the Egyptian state began to allow some measure of political space in society (Hamzawy, interview, 2004). This space began to open up for student activity on university campuses once again, and the political opposition was encouraged by Mubarak's promises of political reform and constitutional change. He loosened state restrictions on syndicates, allowing them a degree of independence from state regulation but without giving them complete autonomy (Choubaky, interview, 2004; Hamzawy, interview, 2004). The lawyers' syndicate was allowed to resume activity after having been disbanded under Sadat as a result of its criticism of Egypt's peace agreement with Israel. The fact that Egypt's diplomatic relations with Israel and America 'had deteriorated' in the early 1980s made it much easier for Mubarak to allow the lawyers' syndicate to resurface; and he did not take any action when it resumed its criticism of the Camp David peace accords in the 1980s (Bianchi, 1989). According to Abul Ella Madi, a former leading figure in the MB, 'it was quite clear that Mubarak in his quest for legitimacy did not foresee syndicates becoming a major sphere of MB activity and source of mobilisation, which would contest state power and hegemony in Egypt' (interview, 2004). Mubarak assumed that the 'corporatist' links between the Egyptian state and the syndicates offered sufficient guarantees of protection from any political forces which might aim to challenge the power and hegemony of the Egyptian state (Fahmy, 2002).

This line of thinking by Mubarak was based on evidence from the presidencies of Nasser and Sadat. However, the 1980s presented a different reality altogether, since the MB was undergoing a process of change in its shape and character which was adding to its political weight in the country, and which resulted in the movement entering the game of syndicate politics (*Al-Ahram*, 7–14 February 2007). The MB's use of syndicates in the 1980s and 1990s became central to its political agenda and to its development into a key political actor in Egypt (Hamzawy, interview, 2004; Choubaky, interview, 2004; Hasan, 2000: 235). In fact, the MB's involvement in syndicates gave it an opportunity to appeal to all sectors of Egyptian society. According to Amr Hamzawy, a leading expert on the MB:

> Through political alliances with political parties, [the MB] was able to appeal to the political elite, through the provision of social services it was able to appeal to the grassroots, strengthening its social base, and its participation in the syndicates gave the MB direct access to the professional class, an important sector in any potential challenge to the power of the Egyptian government, which the MB would launch in the 1990s. (interview, 2004)

Also, according to Abul Ella Madi:

> The MB decided to participate in all democratic institutions, which included professional syndicates, in the 1980s,

so that the MB's ideology could reach a far larger and more important faction of society – middle class professionals – and also to demonstrate the efficiency of the MB in civil activities. (interview, 2004)

The MB's influence over syndicates also provided an important political and social context for experimenting in and demonstrating leadership skills, for enhancing an Islamic sub-culture and for facilitating access to the important middle class (Wickham, 1996; 2002: 179).

The new generation of MB leaders, the syndicates and the Egyptian state

The professional syndicates in Egypt of the 1980s had a number of internal problems which had disabled and paralysed them: internal in-fighting between rival political factions; a lack of transparency; corruption; and financial mismanagement (*Al-Ahram*, 23–29 December 1999; Fahmy, 2002: 137–42). According to Choubaky: 'The professional class had become dissatisfied with the performance of the syndicate boards in dealing with their economic, social and political concerns' (interview, 2004). It was in this failing political and socio-economic context that the MB's pragmatic new leadership entered the syndicates and participated in their elections. The MB candidates for the executive boards of the medical and engineering syndicates ran on an Islamic programme, pushing the slogans of *al-Islam Huwa al-Hal* ('Islam is the solution') and *Na'm Nuriduha Islamiya* ('Yes, we want it to be Islamic') (Choubaky, interview, 2004; Madi, interview, 2004). The syndicate elections featured candidates such as Essam El Eyrian and Abul Futuh, who would become key new-generation activists in the future. The elections in the 1980s of the medical (1984) and engineering (1987) syndicates brought the first victories for the Islamist camp (*Al Ahram*, 18–25 December 1999). The gradual takeover of the syndicates was accompanied by mobilising members to take a more Islamist political position (Madi, interview, 2004; Hamzawy, interview, 2004). The medical and engineering syndicates constituted fertile ground for such activities, given the preponderance of engineering and medical students in the membership of the Islamic Student Movement in the 1970s (Choubaky, interview, 2004; Madi, interview, 2004). Before long, the MB was making inroads into a large number of other syndicates, such as those of the pharmacists, journalists, dentists, scientists, agronomists and commercial employees (*Al Ahram*, 18–25 December 1999). In order to demonstrate the inroads the MB made in the syndicates, the cases of the medical and the engineering syndicates will be examined.

The doctors' syndicate was established in 1920, making it, along with the lawyers', one of the oldest syndicates in Egypt. This longevity adds to the importance of its control and overall management in Egyptian politics. In terms of size, it is relatively small compared to other syndicates, having some 100,000–150,000 registered members (Qandil, 1996: 23), a large percentage of whom are under 35 years of age. This large, young constituency adds to the importance of controlling this syndicate, as it represents the middle class and thus a potential means of challenging the state's authority.

The syndicate has a chairman and a council of 24 members, who oversee the running and management of the syndicate, such as setting its annual budgets and implementing decisions taken by its general assembly (Qandil, interview, 2004). The year 1984 was significant for the syndicate and for the MB, given that the latter secured three seats on the council, giving it a say in the organisation's fundamental operations. This was followed by further success in 1986, indicating a gradual move towards MB domination of the syndicate, and thus towards politicisation and a future challenge to the state's authority (Hamzawy, interview, 2004; Qandil, interview, 2004).

For example, through the syndicate the MB heightened its challenge on a number of political issues, such as the emergency law and corruption in Egyptian politics. As a result the MB was able to win the confidence of the medical constituency, as it was seen as a real contestant of state power, although it first had to clean up the syndicate itself. Its growing influence among the members was strengthened as it improved transparency, providing access to budget statistics and reviews of the council's performance. Such measures had the effect of increasing voter turnout, as rampant internal corruption and concealment had led to dissatisfaction and apathy. Also, as a result of this good management practice, the MB was able to demonstrate its political skills to its secular rivals, which had distrusted it and viewed it as politically incompetent. The MB was thus able to achieve a number of positives through the syndicate, which would have a favourable impact on its performance and perception in the other syndicates.

The engineers' syndicate was established in 1946, and represents approximately 200,000 members. It is governed by a 61-seat council, elected every four years (*Al-Ahram*, 21–27 October 1999; Arafa, September 2001). The syndicate was for a long time (since the 1970s) bound into the state's corporatist structures, when Osman Ahmed Osman, a cousin of Sadat, headed the organisation and aligned it with government policy (Wickham, 2002). The MB would change this, after gaining a presence in the syndicate when they took the chairmanship in 1985 and then gained access to the syndicate's council in 1987, after securing 45 seats. Like the medical syndicate, the MB won the confidence of the engineers' constituency by providing a number of economic services and addressing corruption in the syndicate.

According to Hamzawy, by providing access to affordable economic services and facilities for syndicate members, the MB was able to win confidence in its political agenda and ambitions (Hamzawy, interview, 2004). As a result, it increased the syndicates' politicisation, developing this into a counter-hegemonic challenge to the state. In response to this perceived threat, the government succeeded in placing the syndicate under judicial control, through the introduction in 1993 of Law 100, for alleged financial mismanagement, although it was clear the government's action was politically motivated, the result of the MB's taking control of the syndicate (*Al Ahram*, 11–18 July 2005; Abdul Hafiz, 2003). It remained under judicial control, indicating the government's perception of a continuing threat from, in particular, the MB's influence over its membership (*Al-Ahram*, 13–19 April 2006).

The syndicate had been to a very large extent co-opted into authoritarian state structures, headed as it was during the 1970s by the construction tycoon Osman Ahmed Osman, a friend of Sadat's and related to him by marriage (Wickham, 2002: 186). However, the MB gained a presence for the first time during his term as chairman in 1985, although it did not actually secure a victory until 1987, when it won 45 out of the 61 seats of the council. This was followed by another victory in 1991, with 46 seats (Wickham, 1996; 2002; Hamzawy, interview, 2004; Qandil, interview, 2004). As with other syndicates, the MB won the confidence of its members by providing a wide range of socio-economic services, mainly targeting young members, who accounted for around 35 per cent of the total.

The consolidation of the MB in syndicate politics in the 1980s

The MB's rapid rise in professional syndicates in the 1980s was followed by a policy of consolidation, with the movement aiming to tighten its influence over the professional class. Through its members' positions on councils, the MB tackled socio-economic problems such as corruption and financial mismanagement within the syndicates. Leading MB activists, such as Essam El Eyrian, Abdel Moneim, Abul Futuh and Abul Ella Madi, tackled corruption head on, without regard to personalities or political figures, or to the political parties they might represent in the syndicates (Madi, interview, 2004). This was achieved by the launching of wide-ranging, impressive campaigns against *fasad* (corruption) (Madi, interview, 2004; Choubaky, interview, 2004). According to Choubaky:

> The challenge in dealing with corruption and improving the financial performance of syndicates was assisted by the experience of the new generation, such as individuals like Abul Ella Madi and Essam El Eyrian, from their time on university campuses and involvement in student politics during the 1970s. (interview, 2004)

In addition, the experience of the Islamic Student Movement had provided this new generation of activists with a vast array of political skills, ranging from providing services, calling for an Islamic ideology, challenging different political groups and negotiating with the regime (Madi, interview, 2004; Wickham, 1996; 2002: 117). These skills were instrumental in the MB's success in dealing with corruption and facilitating the provision of social services for their constituents within the syndicates. In the engineers' syndicate, which included almost 200,000 members, the number of those benefiting from the health scheme initiated by the MB increased by 36 per cent (*Al Ahram*, 11–18 July 2005). There was a similar story in the medical syndicate. The MB worked hard to extend medical insurance to syndicate members and their families, to establish social and recreational clubs in rural areas as well as in large cities, to increase the stock of housing available to members at lower prices, and to assist the families of those members arrested or otherwise detained by the Egyptian regime (Madi, interview, 2004; Qandil, interview, 2004; Fahmy, 1998). According to Hamzawy, by such actions, 'the MB syndicate activists renewed the legacy of social Islam pioneered by the pragmatic new generation and allowed the MB to deal with socio-economic problems being faced by the professional class in the syndicates' (interview, 2004). As a result the MB, by securing the support of the professional class, was able to consolidate its position in the syndicates. A rise in turnout for syndicate elections indicated the MB's growing popularity. Table 6.1 demonstrates the rise in registered voters for the doctors' syndicate:

Table 6.1 Trends in Voting Patterns and Number of Candidates in the Medical Syndicate, 1982–92

Year	Total registered voters	Fee-paying members	% of total	Actual number of voters	% of total registered voters	No. of candidates
1982	50,000	20,000	40	2,000	4	34
1984	60,000	30,000	50	6,000	10	85
1986	75,000	40,000	53	11,000	15	59
1988	90,000	50,000	56	12,000	13	62
1990	100,000	65,000	65	21,000	21	130
1992	110,000	70,000	64	30,000	27	180

Source: Qandil, Amany, 'Occupational Groups and Political Participation'. In El Sayid, Mustafa (ed.) *The Reality of Political Pluralism in Egypt*. Cairo: Madbouli, 1996.

In addition to dealing with corruption and financial mismanagement and with the provision of social services, there are a number of other factors which help to explain the consolidation of the MB's position in the syndicates during the 1980s (Madi, interview, 2004; Qandil, interview, 2004). The movement's effective organisation and efficient management of syndicate affairs was central to its success. The MB's decentralised structure and the coordination between its different branches enhanced the efficiency of managing the syndicates, through the exchange of experiences and ideas between the various MB-controlled syndicates (Choubaky, interview, 2004; Qandil, interview, 2004; Al-Awadi, 2004: 67). According to Choubaky and Madi, another key reason is the movement's Islamic appeal (interviews, 2004). Many members of the professional class supported the Islamist bloc, as their members were seen to be respectable, non-corrupt figures, possessing high moral and ethical values – characteristics lacking in their competitors and rival political factions in the syndicates (Wickham, 1996; 2002: 199).

As a result of a combination of and interplay between the above factors, the MB was able first to rise and then quickly to consolidate its position in syndicate politics in Egypt during the 1980s. The movement had created a niche for itself, and a series of episodes in the 1990s further raised its profile in the syndicates. According to Madi:

> These episodes provided the MB with the opportunity to demonstrate their power, through the further politicisation of syndicates, and to mobilise the professional class to challenge the Egyptian state at a time of heightened socio-economic crisis in the 1990s. (interview, 2004)

'These episodes' included the 1991 Gulf War, the MB's victory in the lawyers' syndicate in 1992, and the Egyptian earthquake in 1992 (Madi, interview, 2004; Choubaky, interview, 2004). Each needs an explanation, as they allowed the movement to further their control and politicisation of the syndicates and to mount a direct challenge to the power and structure of the Egyptian state.

The 1991 Gulf War

The MB was quick to condemn Iraq's invasion of Kuwait in 1990, and called for Saddam Hussein to withdraw Iraqi forces in order to end the conflict; this was the same position taken by the Egyptian government. However, Western involvement in the crisis, leading to the bombing of Iraq, led to a break in relations between the MB and the government (Al-Awadi, 2004). The MB used its control over student unions and syndicates to challenge the government's policies of support for the war with Iraq, and of adherence to US policy there.

In response to the government stance, the syndicates controlled by the MB began to form important coalitions to coordinate their actions, and for the first time in their history a 'Committee for Coordinating the Action of Syndicates' was established, in 1990 (Madi, interview, 2004; Al-Awadi, 2004). The idea behind the Committee was not new, having been thought of in the late 1980s, but it was a daring move by the MB, and a provocative one. In an important statement, the Committee condemned the Western military presence in the Gulf and held the Egyptian government responsible for the safety of Egyptians working in Kuwait and Iraq (Madi, interview, 2004; Al-Awadi, 2004). The government responded quickly, forcing the chairmen of those syndicates not controlled by the MB to withdraw from the Committee and to comply with official policy on the Gulf war. Despite this setback, the MB continued its political challenge to the government through the Committee, which went further, in a second statement strongly condemning Egypt's involvement in the war and demanding the return of Egyptian troops (Al-Awadi, 2004).

This had a powerful impact on the government's popular legitimacy, and forced the NDP to declare that Egypt was not a secular but an Islamic state, in a bid to counter the MB's religious discourse. The government also employed the religious institution of Al-Azhar to combat the movement's religious language and imagery (Hamzawy, interview, 2004; Choubaky, interview, 2004). At the same time the MB became a victim of a smear campaign led by the media and by powerful NDP individuals such as Yusuf Wali and Kamal el Shazli, who accused the MB of disloyalty and treason to the Egyptian nation (Al-Awadi, 2004). The syndicates became a concern for the government, and this concern was heightened by the victory of the MB in the influential and politically active lawyers' syndicate, and by its strong presence in other such syndicates.

The MB's success in the lawyers' syndicate

Established in 1912, the lawyers' syndicate was the first professional syndicate in Egypt (Abdul Hafiz, 2003: 24), and has assumed a political role ever since. It has a long history of taking political stands: against British occupation, Nasserite coercive policies, the open-door policy of the 1970s, and restricted liberties under Mubarak (Abdul Hafiz, 2003). The main political factions in the syndicate were the Wafdists, the leftists, the Nasserites and the Islamists. It is noteworthy that the Wafdist lawyers had a very important role in politicising the syndicate, as they controlled it for several decades (Abdul Hafiz, 2003: 75).

In the 1980s, political wrangling between rival political cliques diluted the performance of the lawyers' syndicate in fighting for liberal and national causes, for which it had become famous: by the early 1990s chronic political rivalry had paralysed its council. The MB's new generation of activists, who had gained exposure and credibility through their work on the syndicate's committees on civil liberties and Islamic law, took advantage of the internal political crisis in the elections of 1992 (Madi, interview, 2004; Hamzawy, interview, 2004; Choubaky, interview, 2004). The new generation's superior election campaign, organisation, financing and tactics allowed them to win the support of the lawyers in the syndicate. The new guard organised its candidates on a single national list under the leadership of Sayf al Islam Al Banna, the son of the MB founder Hassan Al Banna. The MB won 18 seats on the executive board and this was echoed by its strong presence on other syndicates known to be political (Wickham, 1996). (Table 6.2 shows the presence of MB members on key syndicate boards in 1992.)

These syndicates were all known for their political activism, in particular the lawyers and, by 1992, the majority of the council members were Islamists, which indicated the growing political power and stature of the MB (see Table 6.2). According to Choubaky, 'the MB began to use its presence in these syndicates

Table 6.2   MB Representation on Councils of Professional Syndicates, 1992

Syndicate	Total no. of council members	No. of Islamists on council
Physicians	25	20
Engineers	61	45
Lawyers	25	18
Pharmacists	25	17

Sources: Qandil, Amany, 'Occupational Groups and Political Participation'. In El Sayid, Mustafa (ed.), *The Reality of Political Pluralism in Egypt*. Cairo: Madbouli, 1996; Qandil, Amany, *The Process of Democratisation in Egypt (1981–1993)*. Cairo: Ibn Khaldun Center for Development Studies, 1995.

in order to address wider economic and political issues in Egypt' (interview, 2004), organising seminars in which political actors from other political parties were invited to participate. Essam El Eyrian, the head of the Medical Association, had been instrumental in making his organisation a national platform for dialogue and discussion relating to all the important economic and political problems that Egypt faced. These seminars addressed key issues such as Islam and secularism, economic reforms, as well as pressing political concerns such as Egypt's role in the Gulf War (Choubaky, interview, 2004; Qandil, interview, 2004; El Diwani, 2003). The MB also held seminars addressing issues such as housing, development, terrorism, freedom, poverty, unemployment and relations with Israel (Madi, interview, 2004; Olav Utvik, 2005). This politicisation of the syndicates in the 1990s by the new-generation leadership reflected the changes taking place in the MB, showing its growing and developing political outlook and confidence. By this process the new leadership significantly transformed the syndicates themselves, making them a vehicle for extending the message of social Islam, defining its larger vision of a centrist Islam, and challenging the hegemony of the Egyptian government, which was already under severe pressure due to the socio-economic crisis of the 1990s, itself the result of economic reform (*Asharq al Awsat*, 27 February 2001; Olav Utvik, 2005).

The Egyptian earthquake

The earthquake of October 1992 was another episode which showed the Egyptian government the political weight of the MB, and so had political implications for the movement. In response to the earthquake the new-generation activists mobilised their resources in the syndicates, as well as in the *tanzim* itself, ensuring a rapid and efficient transfer of resources to the rescue of the earthquake victims (Madi, interview, 2004; Al-Awadi, 2004). This rapid response outmanoeuvred the government, and embarrassed it in the eyes of the public.

The performance of the MB during the earthquake drew praise both in Egypt and abroad, and this seriously concerned the government; Western media noted the contrast between the MB's success and the Egyptian government's relative failure in rescuing the victims and in providing adequate help (Al-Awadi, 2004). President Mubarak was on a visit to China at the time of the disaster, and returned immediately – not only to coordinate efforts in dealing with it, but also because he was concerned at the politicisation of the syndicates and how the MB was using the earthquake to expand its social base and to challenge the government.

The MB used the increased publicity resulting from its relief efforts to promote its Islamic ideology and to mobilise support in syndicates and wider society (Qandil, interview, 2004; Hamzawy, interview, 2004). In the midst of its relief work, the MB displayed banners, on tents and in front of the headquarters of the syndicates under its control, carrying slogans such as 'Islam is the solution' (Madi, interview, 2004). This display of political slogans led to confrontation with the security services, which ordered them to be removed. The medical syndicate complied but others did not, once again caused raising concerns in the government.

The Egyptian state's confrontation with the MB

In reply to the political weight of the MB in the syndicates, which was strengthened as a result of the Gulf War, by its victory in the lawyers' syndicate and by its relief efforts in the earthquake, the Egyptian government made an attempt to understand how the MB was managing to influence the syndicates. The Egyptian government commissioned a number of academics to study and report on MB activity within the syndicates, and in particular what strategies it had used in achieving its successes there. The findings of the report indicated the MB's professionalism, in particular the effective organisation and management which allowed it to run the syndicates efficiently and to address the concerns of the professional class (Qandil, interview, 2004). Soon after this report had been presented to the government, it issued the Associations Law 100, of 16 February 1993, a 'law concerning the assurance of democracy within the syndicates', which was a direct attempt by the Egyptian government to reduce the MB's growing influence (*Al-Ahram*, 21–27 October 1999; Al-Awadi, 2004). The government defended the new law by citing its attempts to increase voter participation and democracy within the syndicates. However, its true objective was clear for all to see: a direct response to the growing role of the MB in the syndicates and in their politicisation, helped as this was by the Gulf War, victory in the lawyers' syndicate (as well control of 19 branches of the lawyers' syndicate in other provinces), and relief for earthquake victims (Choubaky, interview, 2004; Madi, interview, 2004; Qandil, interview, 2004). The new law specified that for the elections to be valid there must be at least a 50 per cent voter turn-out. However, if this mark was not reached, the elections would be held again, and if then a turn-out of 33 per cent was not reached, the syndicate would fall under the administration of officials appointed by the government until such time as new elections were held (Kienle, Spring 1998; Al-Awadi, 2004).

In reaction to this the MB organised demonstrations and work stoppages, drafted petitions to the Speaker of Parliament and sponsored special plenary sessions and joint conferences to mobilise the professional class against Law 100 (Wickham, 1996; 2002). All this failed, however, to force a repeal of the law, but it did make the government realise that it needed to tighten further its control over the syndicates: in February 1995 it introduced new amendments to Law 100, giving extra powers to judges to supervise syndicate elections, as well as to disqualify candidates (Al-Awadi, 2004). When these new amendments also failed in their intended purpose, the Interior Ministry – which had been assigned to enforce the powers of the judges – intervened, halting the syndicate elections on the grounds that the Islamist candidates belonged to an outlawed movement. This involved Essam El Eyrian in the medical syndicate in 1995, and Sayf al Islam Al Banna in the lawyers' syndicate in 1996 (Madi, interview, 2004). In addition to this, following a court case over financial irregularities, the engineers' syndicate was placed under the supervision of judges until another date was set for the elections (*Al-Ahram*, 21–27 October 1999). The new-generation MB leadership saw the timing of the case as an orchestrated campaign to stop them winning seats in the elections, and as a result refused to comply with the court's ruling (Al-Awadi, 2004). When the security forces broke into the syndicate to enforce the ruling and suspended the council, which was dominated by the MB, it filed an appeal in the courts against the government's action. The arrests and trials of members of the medical, lawyers' and engineers' syndicates confirmed that the government was overtly concerned by the MB's use of syndicates as political platforms in order to challenge the power of the state (Choubaky, interview, 2004; Madi, interview, 2004). Furthermore, what occurred in the engineers' syndicate showed that the new-generation activists would not easily give up what they had worked towards and achieved in the syndicates. According to Hamzawy:

This reflected the broader spirit in the new generation, which emphasised the fact that the MB should not be deterred from its progress in influencing syndicates and politics but should aim to expand that influence further to weaken the hegemony of the Egyptian state. (interview, 2004)

Therefore, despite the government crackdown, the new generation stepped up their demands for political and constitutional reforms. Importantly, they continued to use syndicates as venues for meetings and seminars, thus maintaining their political significance (Madi, interview, 2004). For example, according to Qandil:

The MB's new generation continued to use their skills as organisers and alliance builders to develop support for their political demands in the syndicates, not only amongst the professional class but also with political activists of varying political affiliations (interview, 2004).

A two-day conference on 'Freedoms and Civil Society' was held in October 1994 at the medical association, organised by Essam El Eyrian and Abul Ella Madi, bringing together hundreds of prominent activists and intellectuals, including government figures, to hammer out a consensus on basic rights (Choubaky, interview, 2004). A delegation from the conference, including the two co-organisers, visited the Nobel laureate Naguib Mahfouz in hospital to express their high-profile support and their condemnation of his stabbing by militant Islamists. At the same time, the MB were issuing communiqués condemning every attack by militant Islamists on tourists and government figures, and even brokered a ceasefire deal between the radical Islamists and the government during the UN's Population Conference in Cairo (Choubaky, interview, 2004; Qandil, interview, 2004).

These moves by the MB to build support for its demands and to remove the restrictions on the syndicates led to pressure being brought to bear on the government, which in 2001 rescinded judicial control of the lawyers' syndicate and allowed free elections (*Al-Ahram*, 10–16 March 2005). These were won by the MB in a sweeping victory: it secured all but one of the 24 council seats (Choubaky, interview, 2004; *Asharq al Awasat*, 27 February 2001; Arafa, September 2001). However, the post of chairman was won by the Nasserite Sameh Ashour, a famous opponent of the MB, and the resultant tension between him and the council was unfortunately reflected in inefficiency in dealing with syndicate affairs. Early in 2005 new elections took place; and Ashour won his seat again, while the MB was reduced to 15 seats (*Al-Ahram*, 24–30 March 2005). The MB accused the government of interfering in the election process and of rigging the election for the benefit of their ally Ashour, and filed a lawsuit contesting the results (*Al-Ahram*, 24–30 March 2005). Despite allowing syndicate elections to take place, the government thus continued with its policy of interference in syndicate affairs in order to curb the power of the MB. This has been explained by El Eyrian, who believes that the paralysis of the syndicates was a result of the MB's political challenge to the Egyptian government:

> They want to stop [us] from presenting an example of effectuality and from reaching a strong podium to air our political views in the absence of political life. But our success was obvious from 1984 and 1985 when we first appeared. The syndicate here was nothing but two rooms where very little work was done. Today our activities have reached all corners of the globe. Wherever we go, from Afghanistan to Iraq, we show the true face of Egypt. They fear our success, and they don't want us to show our abilities. The Brotherhood was able to gain the trust of a broad section of the Egyptian people. Despite the campaign against Islam and against Islamic movements, the Brotherhood continues to win any elections because of this trust. (*Egypt Today*, June 2006)

In addition El Eyrian believes that the Egyptian state inflicted much more harm on itself than on the MB by its control of the syndicates. 'This is going to make [the government's] image even worse in front of the rest of the world,' he explained, adding that:

> All reform initiatives talk about civil society and the importance of encouraging civil work. Professional and labour syndicates are the backbone of civil society. And what has the government done? It has nationalized labour syndicates, frozen professional syndicates and paralysed the actions of NGOs. It looks very bad. Now the government wants to beautify itself with nominal changes. It's ridiculous. Our stance as professionals is clear: Law 100 must be cancelled and syndicates should be left to their members, to be run according to their own internal laws. (*Egypt Today*, June 2006)

According to Hamzawy, 'the Egyptian government is unlikely to change its policy towards professional syndicates any time soon, given the rise of the MB in the Egyptian parliament, and its increased social base in Egypt' (interview, 2004). Through the syndicates the movement was able to demonstrate its political weight to the government, and its ability to address critical socio-economic issues, which put pressure on the government at a time of economic crisis (Hamzawy, interview, 2004; Choubaky, interview, 2004). Though the MB continued to exist and to work in the syndicates, the latter's effectiveness in challenging state power was weakened as a result of the government's coercive legislation. In reaction to this the movement, and in particular the pragmatic new generation, searched for new avenues through which to challenge the government. A new weapon in the MB's armoury was its willingness to form alliances with civil groups and other organisations, an indication of its desire to drive through further changes in the character of the movement. This came to prominence up to and after the 2005 presidential and parliamentary elections, and increased the MB's political weight – it gave it the ability to extend its social base, and to make it more diverse and more political in nature and outlook through courting alterantive political constituencies.

The new generation: from syndicates to civilian alliances

'We simply have no choice but to reform,' the MB's Second Deputy Supreme Guide Khairat El-Shater wrote in a commentary entitled 'No Need to be Afraid of Us', in the *The Guardian* newspaper, in response to the MB's success in the 2005 parliamentary election runoffs (*Al Ahram*, 24–30 November 2005; 15–21 December 2005). El-Shater went further, in defining the MB's goal as 'to end the monopoly cf government by a single party and boost popular engagement in political activity' (*Al Ahram*, 24–30 November 2005). At a point only halfway through the second stage of the 2005 parliamentary elections, the MB had already secured 24.6 per cent of the seats contested, against its target of 100 (22.5 per cent) cut of a total of 444. However, unlike the 1984 and 1987 elections, when alliances existed in the context of the party system, nearly two decades later coalitions involving the MB had moved beyond that context and acted more along the lines of civilian activism. This represented a move by the MB's new generation of leaders to find fresh avenues of opposition to the state, given that civil institutions such as syndicates had been weakened by state intervention. As a result the leadership formed a strong alliance with the *Kefayah* movement in the period leading up to and after the 2005 presidential and parliamentary elections. *Kefayah* is a movement which rose to become a powerful voice, of Egyptian civilians of different political backgrounds and persuasions who came to a consensus on the need for economic and political change in Egypt. The strength of the MB alliance with *Kefayah* was shown by the fact that the latter's manifesto reflected the political demands which were being made by the MB. *Kefayah's* understanding of political reform was similar to that of the MB – the 'termination of the current monopoly of power at all levels, starting with the seat of the President of the Republic' (as defined in their manifesto). Furthermore *Kefayah*, like the MB, aimed to break the hold of the ruling party on power and all its instruments – it sought the repeal of the Emergency Law and of all other laws which constrain public and individual freedoms. It also sought constitutional reforms that would allow direct election of the president and vice-presidents from among several candidates, as well as limiting their period in office to two terms, the reform of parliamentary elections, freedom of association and freedom of the press. *Kefayah* and the MB thus undeniably shared common policies, and therefore made common cause. As Wael Khalil – a socialist and *Kefayah* activist – articulated in *Al-Ahram Weekly*, 'The Muslim Brotherhood is, without question, my ally [in the battle for reform] … [Government] thugs attacked voters and innocent citizens and we're confident about the Muslim Brotherhood's commitment to a civil state' (24–30 November, 2005).

The MB's alliance with *Kefayah* was indicative of the willingness on the part of the former's new-generation activists to cross ideological barriers in seeking to boost the movement's social and political power. The pragmatic new leadership was comfortable with this alliance, given its past experience of making other such alliances with political parties and organisations of different political persuasions. It was difficult for the government to deal with this shifting nature of the MB; the movement's flexibility was a key factor in allowing it to build political power and weight, and generally to make life difficult for the government. Given the clear political role which the MB developed for itself in Egypt, through participation in the parliament and syndicates, and through forming alliances (both political and civil), it put the government on the back foot. This was even more dangerous for the government, as it attempted to deal with the growing socio-economic crisis and to manage the process of political succession in Egypt.

Conclusion

This chapter has explored the role of professional syndicates in the quest of the MB's pragmatic new leadership to build up its power, and to challenge the hegemony of the Egyptian government at a time of socio-economic crisis in the 1990s. It took in the MB's entry into syndicates in the 1980s, and how it was able to rise quickly, resulting in its domination of the syndicate councils. This success provided the movement with the opportunity to use the syndicates as tools with which to challenge the government, and was given additional impetus in the 1990s by the Gulf War, victory in the lawyers' syndicate, and the MB's relief efforts in the aftermath of the 1992 earthquake. These episodes allowed the MB to politicise the syndicates and to use them for political ends, which in turn led to a crackdown by the Egyptian government, whose political strategy began to evolve around the perceived political threats and challenges from the MB. The MB continued to have a bearing on the government's political strategy especially as the politics of a succession process came to the fore. It is therefore important to explore the politics of that process, taking into consideration the actors involved, and to examine the key political actors, such as the MB, in the context of their influence and impact on the succession.

7

THE POLITICS OF
SUCCESSION: THE RISE OF
GAMAL MUBARAK

This book has so far examined the process of economic and political reform in Egypt and the overall impact of that reform on the MB, which allowed it to develop into a key political actor and in the 1990s to mount a challenge to the government. Central to this challenge was the MB's changing shape and character, which allowed it to contest state power through its presence in parliament and in professional syndicates. This led to repressive action by the state, but the MB was able to survive the offensive because it had a presence both inside and outside the system, making it difficult for the government to deal with the challenges it posed. In reaction to the MB's political weight, the government, to ensure its own survival, had to pursue a careful process of managing socioeconomic and political demands, and after 2000 to be shrewd in the way it handled the process of political succession. This represents a major political development in Egypt in recent years, one that requires exploring and unpacking. This chapter thus examines how the government managed the process of political succession, through introducing controlled economic and political reform, and provides an understanding of the process of 'grooming' of the actors and forces involved in the state-managed process of political succession in Egypt. It will also examine key political actors such as the military and the MB in terms of their influence on that process.

The economic and political grooming of Gamal Mubarak

Gamal Mubarak, son of the Egyptian President, Hosni Mubarak, had worked as a banker and investor in London until his return to Cairo in 1996. His banking and financial skills gave him the much-needed credentials of a potential manager and reformer of the ailing Egyptian economy. Also, his liberal economic outlook inspired confidence and support from the influential business community within and beyond the confines of Egypt (*Washington Post*, 17 December 2003; *Al Jazeera*, 29 March 2005). Gamal's first significant appointment was in 1997, to the US–Egypt president's council. At that time this was a prominent body which brought together business people from the two countries. The contacts Gamal made in this important sector have expanded over time, for example through presentations and attendance at various business associations, including the influential American-Egyptian Chamber of Commerce, and affiliation with economic think-tanks (most visibly USAID) funded by the Egyptian Centre for Economic Studies, all of which contributed to his network of contacts with the business class (Zenati, 2004).

Gamal's political packaging was handled in an equally strategic fashion. The initial step was to present Gamal Mubarak as a champion of youth, a category of citizens who have suffered disproportionately from poverty and unemployment (Nafa, interview, 2004; El Said, interview, 2004). If ignored, unemployed youth could pose a most serious threat to economic and political stability in Egypt. The Future Generation Foundation was created by the government to provide a vehicle through which the problems of disaffected youth could be addressed (Ghobashy, 2003). The growth of the foundation raised suspicions among the political opposition that it would be used by Gamal as a platform to run for the presidency; by 2000, however, it was clear that these suspicions were unfounded. In January 2000, he joined the NDP's General Secretariat, and at the September 2002 party conference was elected head of the policy secretariat, which quickly became the NDP's key decision-making body (*BBC News*, 29 September 2003). The secretariat was charged with the task of formulating NDP policy and modernising the party; its mandate extended to reviewing legislation before it was submitted to parliament. The secretariat had 200 members, but it was apparent that the process of decision-making lay in the hands of a small group closely associated with Gamal (*Al Ahram*, 23–29 September 2004). For example, Gamal as head of the secretariat seeded the NDP with his followers, among whom were his spin doctor, political scientist Aly Eldin Helal; Ahmed Ezz, a multi-millionaire businessman known as the 'emperor of iron'; Rachid Mohammed Rachid, the Minister of Foreign Trade and Industry; and Mahmoud Mohieddin, the Minister of Investment, who led the process of privatisation.

Gamal's appointment to the new policy secretariat coincided with a spate of corruption cases against former ministers and high-ranking officials. This was cunningly used by Gamal to project an image of himself as a reformer and moderniser, and was also a political move to marginalise the NDP's powerful old guard, who had dominated the party for decades (*Al Ahram*, 20–26 October 2005). For example, the right-hand man to Youssef Wali, a veteran old-guard NDP powerhouse, was charged with accepting bribes to import carcinogenic French pesticides into Egypt. At the party congress, Youssef Wali was ejected from his post as the party's secretary-general and replaced by Information Minister Safwat al-Sherif (Ghobashy, 2003). Within the space of a few months, Gamal had become substantially more influential over policy issues than the Prime Minister. The ambiguity surrounding the exact role and powers of the policy secretariat triggered a wave of criticism, particularly within opposition circles. Some considered it tantamount to a secret society within the party, while others described it as a centre of power that operated behind closed doors. Political pundits agreed that the policy secretariat had become the NDP's political backbone. According to Hussein Abdel-Razeq, the leftist *al Tagammu* party's assistant secretary-general, the September 2002 NDP congress was mandated to place Gamal Mubarak at the helm of power. 'It is now clear,' said Abdel-Razeq, 'that the Policy Secretariat was created especially for [Gamal] Mubarak to lead, and has been transformed into Egypt's supreme policy-making body' (*Al Ahram*, 15–21 May 2003). Nabil Abdel Fattah, an expert in civil society and Islamic movements at the Al-Ahram Center for Political and Strategic Studies, believed that the NDP had effectively been reduced to the policy secretariat, and that the danger lay in the fact that the secretariat's members wielded power without legitimacy: they were unelected, and had not earned their position by any clear demonstration of political expertise (Abdel Fattah, interview, 2004). Nor did Abdel Fattah believe the secretariat had made progress in its mission of modernising the NDP; rather, the policy secretariat failed to develop the party's internal infrastructure, or to challenge conservative and dogmatic ideas long dominant within the party. The endgame was not so much about modernising the party but about creating a launch pad for the President's son to enter the political scene, from where he could present his economic and political strategy for the future of the country (el Abdel Fattah, interview, 2004).

Gamal also vested energy in harnessing support from Washington for the intended succession. Gamal was put in charge of high-level delegations to the US capital on two occasions during 2003. On these excursions Gamal met with senior US officials, such as Vice-President Dick Cheney (Ghobashy, 2003; Middle East Media and Research Institute, 8 July 2003). He was also chosen as the source to reveal the news that Washington was pressing the Egyptian government to announce political reform, or the news was timed to coincide with his visits. The release of the American University in Cairo professor Saad Eddin Ibrahim immediately preceded

Gamal's first Washington visit of the year, as did a statement of willingness to meet with Israeli Prime Minister Ariel Sharon. News of the abolition of the penal code's hard labour penalty and of the creation of a national council for human rights was released by Gamal through the NDP policy secretariat (Nafa, interview, 2004; El Said, interview, 2004). The clear message intended by these steps was that Gamal was willing to make concessions to the US in the areas of foreign policy, human rights and liberal economic reform, a picture which boosted Egypt's image in the US, and portrayed Gamal as a reformer and moderniser in the context of economic and political reform.

All this helped in packaging Gamal to appeal to the Egyptian desire for much-needed economic and political reform (Middle East Media and Research Institute, 24, 25 July 2000). He spoke frequently of the need for reform, especially of the ruling party. The NDP had a bad image among the Egyptian people, being viewed as an ageing and out-of-date organisation run by an autocratic leadership concerned with self-interest rather than with genuine economic and political reform. Gamal's repeated calls for 'new faces', especially younger people, to enter the party, parliament and the political elite more generally, reinforced by his visible association with a relatively young circle (aged 45–60) of technocrats and businessmen, promoted the perception that with Gamal a new generation of Egyptians would take power – a generation interested in pushing forward real economic and political reforms in the country (*Al Ahram*, 5–11 August 2004).

Devout Muslims, a vital constituency, were not left off Gamal's agenda. The run-up to the invasion of Iraq in March 2003 saw the NDP coordinating anti-war demonstrations with the religious institution of Al-Azhar and the influential MB. The objective was to develop religious legitimacy through these organisations, even though the government had been consistently fearful of either of them growing in strength and posing a challenge to the state and to the succession process (Nafa, interview, 2004; El Said, interview, 2004). It is thus apparent that no constituency of society seen as vital was missed in the economic and political grooming of Gamal. The businessmen, the technocrats, the religious bodies and the Egyptian people themselves were all addressed directly or indirectly by Gamal. Nor was the military overlooked, as the principal arbiter and guarantor of regime stability in Egypt. Gamal's courting of this institution was an ongoing process after his return to Egypt in 1996. Every president since the July 1952 revolution had come from the military establishment, and the consent and support of the military, the backbone of the Egyptian state, was vital for the government to manage the process of political succession (Nafa, interview, 2004; El Said, interview, 2004).

Despite what seems clearly to have been a process of grooming, the NDP was quick to dismiss rumours circulating around the country linking Gamal and the political succession. In September 2002 presidential adviser Osama El Baz told *Newsweek* that 'Gamal Mubarak is not running for any official office. He is interested in public issues, like any young man interested in the future of his country, but he is not going to pursue any official position' (17 October 2002). In May 2003 Gamal himself told an audience of 600 at his alma mater, the American University in Cairo, that:

> There are rumours that I am being groomed for the post, but they are baseless and have nothing to do with reality. Scaling down my activities is not an option; I want to encourage the youth to be active and I will not alter the role I believe in (*Al Ahram*, 8–14 May 2003).

The following month Gamal was asked on US television whether he would be Egypt's president one day. He told the interviewer:

> The issue is not to try and personalise the process of change; the issue is to focus on the process and to shed light on the reality of Egypt today. A lot of young Egyptians are

stepping forward to play a leading role in shaping the future
(*World Talk*, 26 June 2003).

In spite of the denials expressed in statements by senior NDP
officials and by Gamal himself, the Egyptian opposition was not
persuaded. They saw these emphatic denials as effectively signal-
ling that a path was being smoothed for the political succession of
Gamal. Political developments post-2004 further persuaded the
opposition that Gamal was indeed being prepared to succeed his
father at some point in the near future.

The economic and political strengthening of Gamal Mubarak: the 2004 cabinet reshuffle and the 2005 presidential and parliamentary elections

To many political analysts, the evidence of Gamal's growing power
increased after the cabinet reshuffle in July 2004 (*BBC News*, 14
July 2004). Critics of the dynastic inheritance of power believed
that Hosni Mubarak had smoothed Gamal's path to the presidency
by using the reshuffle to place his son's close colleagues in key positions (Abdel Fattah, interview, 2004; El Said, interview, 2004).
One opposition newspaper ran the headline 'Gamal Mubarak's
Government' (*Al Ahram*, 15–21 July 2004). The cabinet, once
largely composed of diehard NDP members, was now studded
with young, Western-educated individuals who shared Gamal's
liberal vision of economic reform (*Al Ahram*, 15–21 July 2004;
5–11 August 2004; 23–29 September 2004). Seven of the new
ministers appointed in the cabinet reshuffle also served on Gamal's
influential policy secretariat, which formulated policy for the NDP.
Three of the new ministers were referred to as his 'lieutenants'
in the media. Many reflected his ethos: they were young, savvy,
reform-minded economic technocrats, from academia or business, who had worked or studied abroad (El Said, interview, 2004;
Nafa, interview, 2004). For example, Mahmoud Mohieddin, a
former Minister for Investment, obtained his doctorate from

Warwick University, and the credentials of Mohammed Rachid, former Minister for Foreign Trade and Investment, include advanced management studies at Stanford, MIT and Harvard. Hani Shukrallah, the former editor of *Al-Ahram* weekly, described Gamal and his reformists as follows:

> They are modernists, more fluent in English and other languages, educated abroad, belonging to the younger generation. They are more open to Western management techniques, more exposed to Western culture and definitely economic liberals (*NBC News*, 28 July 2004).

The reshuffle was evident not only at the governmental level but within other sectors, such as banking, finance and the media. For example, it was noticeable in Cairo after 2004 that the three economic Ministries and the Central Bank were recruiting a large number of young, Western-educated staff members to drive the process of economic reform, in particular the process of privatisation (Nafa, interview, 2004; El Said, interview, 2004; Cunningham, 2005). These new appointments tightened Gamal's grip on power, and this was enhanced by the results of the 2005 presidential and parliamentary elections.

Gamal was a guiding force behind his father's campaign for Egypt's first-ever multi-candidate presidential elections in September 2005 (*Arab News*, 30 September 2005). He was ever-present behind the scenes at presidential events, while not himself addressing audiences or the media. The presidential campaign team was put together by Gamal and his reformists, assembling in the process a 103-strong team of politicians and media advisors to secure victory for his father. The team included, for example, Lamees al Hadidi, a 38 year old charismatic former *NBC* and *New York Times* reporter, and Dina al Imam, a reader in political science at UCLA, Berkeley (*Daily Telegraph*, 4 September 2005). The polished campaign tactics, including US-style gimmickry and presidential advertisements, all emphasised the influence of Gamal on his father's presidential strategy and campaigning. After the presidential elections, Gamal further stamped his authority on the country at the annual NDP conference in September 2005, declaring his camp's victory over the old guard in the party. In a keynote speech to members of the NDP, Gamal took much of the credit for his father's electoral landslide, and set the tone for the parliamentary elections that followed in November: 'During the presidential elections, the party proved its ability to modernise, proved the worth of the ideas it has been promoting since the party took a new orientation in 2002' (*Arab News*, 30 September 2005).

The conference had been billed as a watershed in the party, with Gamal gaining new prominence after masterminding his father's 2005 presidential victory. The conference not only consolidated the position of the reformers within the party but saw them push the old guard aside. Through the presidential elections and the NDP conference Gamal built up momentum, which he then used in the parliamentary elections. Gamal launched the NDP's parliamentary election campaign in Cairo on 29 October 2005, at a gathering in front of the Abideen presidential palace in Cairo for the presentation of the NDP's Cairo candidates. The list of NDP candidates for the parliamentary elections included 176 newcomers, reflecting Gamal's influence in introducing fresh faces to parliament. It was made clear by the presence of Mohammed Kamal, a key associate of Gamal and a member of his presidential campaign team (*Al Ahram*, 29 September–5 October; 20–26 October 2005). This dominant role played by Gamal in the presidential and parliamentary elections did not escape the attention of the Egyptian opposition. Ayman Nour of *al Ghad* party contended that the Egyptian government was preparing Gamal's succession by turning the NDP, with its hold on patronage and the government bureaucracy, into his personal vehicle to power, and that the influence and power of Gamal had become so extensive over the previous year that he was effectively running the country by proxy (*Washington Post*, 24 September 2005).

Following the 2005 elections Gamal Mubarak and his associates continued to exercise influence in the NDP, whether in the context of the NDP's organisation or in the direction of economic strategy. They dominated the annual NDP conferences, defending the country's economic strategy, in particular privatisation and the role of the business class. Gamal's appointment as Deputy Secretary-General of the party was further evidence of his grooming and of the influence which he had come to exercise over the NDP and the political world in Egypt, in particular over his father. Gamal Mubarak was quick to make statements on crucial regional issues and headed a number of important delegations, notably to Lebanon and the US, which were usually reserved for the head of state or the Foreign Minister. Thus he had put himself firmly in place to succeed his father, despite denials. However, he still faced obstacles in the form of political competitors (both military and civilian), who stood as challenges to his quest for the presidency of Egypt.

The politics of succession in Egypt: Gamal Mubarak's challengers and competitors

Gamal Mubarak had been singled out as the only real contender to take over from his father – naturally enough, given the continuous process of grooming he had undergone, in both economics and politics, since 1996. Despite this ever-increasing focus upon Gamal, one widely-mentioned name as his competitor was that of Umar Sulaiman, Mubarak's head of Egyptian General Intelligence (*BBC News*, 14 July 2004). Prior to 2002, Sulaiman's name was not widely known inside Egypt, although it is fair to say that it was familiar to those interested and concerned with Egyptian security and with the on-going Egyptian mediation in the Israeli-Palestinian crisis (El Said, interview, 2004; Nafa, interview, 2004). Publicity and visibility were therefore important for building Sulaiman's profile and familiarising him to the Egyptian public. As a result of this lack of awareness in Egyptian society, Sulaiman began to play a more visible role, renouncing the previously clandestine nature of his presence in Egypt, allowing his name to become well known and, importantly, giving him a platform for constructing a possible challenge for the presidency. His photographs appeared in the newspapers, and previously secretive diplomatic missions to Palestine were publicised, to emphasise his importance in dealing with the Palestinian issue. The Americans and the Europeans had come to acknowledge the important role of Sulaiman in Egypt, in particular in relation to the ever-important issues of Egyptian and regional security. Given the post-9/11 security climate, Sulaiman's cooperation became more important for the Americans, with Egypt seen as playing a crucial role in assisting in the Iraqi crisis and mediating in the Palestinian crisis (El Said, interview, 2004; el Abdel Fattah, interview, 2004).

Umar Sulaiman can be seen to have had a broad appeal and influence over key institutions in Egypt. He was a key figure among the Egyptian security elite in dealing and negotiating with the various Islamist organisations, in particular during the 1980s and 1990s when Egypt was facing an insurgency from such organisations intent on taking over the country. Given this experience, Sulaiman appeared to be an ideal candidate to handle Islamist issues; the alternative would be to introduce someone new, without his level of insight into Islamism and his knowledge of Islamist organisations (El Said, interview, 2004). Like the Minister of Defence Hussein Tantawi, Umar Sulaiman participated in the 1967 and 1973 wars with Israel, which did him no harm in courting high-ranking military officers also involved in past wars. A potential problem for him however was his role as head of the Egyptian intelligence service, owing to its history of disputes with the powerful military. The conflict and rivalry between these two central security institutions could hinder Sulaiman's chances, as the backing and support of the military, given its strength and influence in Egyptian politics, made it more important than the intelligence sector (el Abdel Fattah, interview, 2004; Nafa, interview, 2004; El Said, interview, 2004). Sulaiman, in order to be a genuine competitor to Gamal Mubarak, needed to adopt a cautious balance between the two, and avoid alienating or undermining the military.

Some of those familiar with the Egyptian and Russian political and security scene drew comparisons between Sulaiman and Putin, given that Putin took over the presidency in Russia after a successful career in the KGB. Although a similarity may be drawn between the careers of Sulaiman and Putin, the institutional power of the Egyptian military was much greater than that of the intelligence service (El Said, interview, 2004; Nafa, interview, 2004). Also, a Putin-like concentration of power in the centre, an economic policy directed towards nationalisation and a campaign of harassment and arrest of oligarchs would not have strengthened Sulaiman's credentials among the Egyptian business elite or global financial institutions. One could argue, furthermore, that it is overly simplistic to draw parallels with the experience of Russia under Putin, as Egypt had stronger relations with international donors such as the IMF and WB, making a reversal of Egypt's liberal economic reforms a somewhat unrealistic prospect, as compared to Russia (El Said, interview, 2004).

The sudden emergence of Umar Sulaiman into the Egyptian political world was viewed by some as a carefully thought out strategy by Hosni Mubarak to prevent moves by another military officer to compete with Gamal, rather than seriously viewing Sulaiman as a contender for the presidency. The President's age, and the reports of his on-going illnesses post 2003, strengthened this suspicion that Umar Sulaiman was being used as a pawn to prevent the military from presenting their candidate, while attempting to comfort them by pushing Umar Sulaiman, himself a former military officer, as a prospective Vice-President (El Said, interview, 2004; Abdel Fattah, interview, 2004). The backing of the military is extremely significant, and a name touted by some commentators, although not as prominently as that of Umar Sulaiman, was Magdi Hatata, who was Chief of Staff of the Egyptian armed forces, but lacked public profile at that time. There were more dynamic high-ranking officers with greater popularity than Magdi Hatata, but all of them faced the same obstacle, which was that none had a clear constitutional path to the presidency.

Regarding a possible civilian challenge in the politics of succession, the Egyptian government was shrewd in the way it sidelined any civilian competition to Gamal Mubarak. It used its power to reshuffle the political elite, removing popular individuals while keeping highly disliked personalities in place. The government also created constitutional barriers for civilian candidates, thus effectively removing possible civilian challengers from the succession process (El Said, interview, 2004; el Abdel Fattah, interview, 2004). The two most popular members of the cabinet over the past decade, Ahmad al Guwalli and Amr Mussa, were both transferred to the Arab League, where they had no direct access to the Egyptian public or political elite (Shehata, 2002). This process of removing popular personalities from public life is similar to how Hosni Mubarak acted in the 1990s, when the highly popular Field Marshal Abdel al Halim Abu Ghazzala was placed under house arrest for more than a decade. Abu Ghazzala's popularity was a constant threat to the legitimacy of Mubarak, which led to the former being marginalised from the public (Nafa, interview, 2004; El Said, interview, 2004). The position of Minister of the Interior was frequently rotated, and Habib al Adli, for example, was a rather dour technocrat with a background in state security, not a career which brought him public admiration. His public rapport was further weakened through demands for his resignation after the assault in 2005 on women journalists by security officials, as they were demonstrating against the 25 May referendum on the amendment of the constitution's Article 76. Neither were Speaker of Parliament, Fathi Surur, or the previous Prime Minister, Atif

Obeid, held in high esteem by the public (El Said, interview, 2004). In the 1990s Obeid oversaw controversial economic reforms which worsened the socio-economic crisis in Egypt. Mubarak's Minister of Defence, General Tantawi, seemed relatively anonymous, which was a serious weakness. The 65-year-old general, a veteran of the Arab-Israeli wars in 1956, 1967 and 1973, was frequently at Hosni Mubarak's side, and on occasion stood in for him at official events such as the 30th anniversary of the death of Nasser, in September 2000 (*Al Hayat*, 28 September 2000).

Among the constitutional barriers erected by the government to deter civilian challengers was the revision of Article 76, which presented a major barrier: it stipulated that independent candidates would need the support of a minimum of 250 members in governmental institutions such as the Shura Council, the People's Assembly and local councils (*BBC News*, 20 May 2005). This was a difficult task as these institutions were dominated by pro-government and NDP members – for example, human-rights activist Saad Eddin Ibrahim was deterred from entering the presidential race in 2005.

It was thus apparent that the government had implemented a number of tactics to marginalise any challenges to the state-managed process of political succession. The jailing of the charismatic Ayman Nour, ruling him out as a competitor of Gamal Mubarak, was a clear example of this (*Arab News*, 25 December 2005). However, despite the state's management of the succession process, there were political actors in Egypt, such as the military and the MB, which had an interest in influencing that process and, in this respect both posed dilemmas for the government. In Egypt the military were a key institution and the MB had considerable political weight, making it difficult for the state to sideline these two actors or prevent them from having a say in the politics of succession.

The role of the Egyptian military in the political succession of Gamal Mubarak

The question of the military has always been linked to the issue of succession, given the prominent role the institution played in Egyptian political life since the 1952 revolution. It is fair to say that Gamal constructed a comfortable niche for himself, but could not be comprehensively secure without the consent and approval of the military (Abdel Fattah, interview, 2004; El Said, interview, 2004). The fact that Gamal was not an officer – indeed has no military experience – posed certain dilemmas for the military hierarchy, in particular as to whether Gamal would secure its interests. This was not a problem under Nasser, Sadat or Hosni Mubarak, as they all came from the ranks of the military. Although a more civilian cabinet emerged under Sadat and Mubarak, both continued to safeguard the economic and political interests of the military (Harb, 2003). The latter, in return, acted as a guarantor of security for the government, which turned to the army on several occasions during the 1970s and 1980s to deal with internal political instability – it had to be relied upon to deal with the bread riots in 1977 and with Islamic radicalism in the 1980s (Sid Ahmed, 1987–88). There was an element of trust and understanding between previous Egyptian governments and the military, whereby the latter guaranteed state security and in return their interests were taken care of.

This trust factor was crucial for the military to back Gamal's succession, and the government was fully aware of this; the succession process was managed to avoid raising eyebrows within the military hierarchy (El Said, interview, 2004; Nafa, interview, 2004). For example, the government initially began to package Gamal Mubarak as a champion of Egyptian youth through the establishment of the Future Generation Foundation. However, this way of pushing Gamal into the public domain did not receive the backing of high-ranking officers, who saw the tactic as an effort to marginalise the military – undermining their authority by failing to approach them beforehand. When this came to the notice of the government a new method of presenting Gamal to the public was sought, and since this episode, with its rumours of displeasure in the military, Gamal Mubarak was careful to court support in military circles, especially among those younger military officers who held significant and prominent positions (Sobelman, 2001).

A key factor for Gamal Mubarak in his quest to take over from his father was the US, which already seemed to approve of Gamal as the next leader of Egypt. The US, a key Egyptian ally and a major aid donor, had a high level of influence in Egyptian politics, and so could be a factor in determining the succession process (*Al Dostur*, 11 August 2006; Sobelman, 2001). The former US ambassador to Israel, Martin Indyk, pointed out that the political succession process common among Arab regimes has been in line with a US policy of political continuity, as reflected by the successful transmission of power in Jordan, Morocco and Bahrain, and by the close ties that have linked late rulers' sons with American institutions (*Al Ahram*, 7–13 October 1999). Given this policy it seemed almost inevitable that the US would work to mend any fences between Gamal and the military, to help the Egyptian government secure a smooth succession process. Gamal had been well marketed to the Americans as an energetic young civilian of the new entrepreneurial class, with global views and with business interests in the US itself. This was very attractive to policy makers in Washington, and there was no doubt of the importance of US views in swinging the sceptics in the Egyptian military towards supporting Gamal Mubarak in his mission to take up the presidency (*Al Dostur*, 11 August 2006).

The military, central to Egyptian security, and consequently its influence on the political succession process was evident, albeit only behind closed doors and within the strategic strata of Egyptian politics. Alongside the military, meanwhile, there were alternative political actors who were also trying to influence the succession process, and there was vocal criticism of the government-managed process by the political opposition, in particular the MB. Given that the movement constituted a key player in Egyptian politics, it is important to explore what impact it was able to have, if any, on the succession process in Egypt.

The MB's influence on the political succession process in Egypt

There is no doubt that the politics of succession became a major talking point in Egypt in recent years, and generated much criticism and opposition in Egyptian society. In particular, the process as managed by the government met with strong opposition from the MB. The reasons for this opposition were not consistent, with divergent views from the orthodox old guard and the pragmatic new generation of MB activists (El Said, interview, 2004; Nafa, interview, 2004). The latter opposed the succession process because in their view the politics of succession represented a manipulation of the political system and a major setback to the process of political change leading to democracy in Egypt (*Al Hayat*, 28 September 2000). Purely political reasoning thus underpinned the new generation's resistance to the government-managed succession process in Egypt. On the other hand, the old guard, more orthodox in their understanding of Islam, opposed the process from a different standpoint – that of Islamic legitimacy. According to orthodox Sunni Islam, a leader without the consent of the people is illegitimate, and the inheritance of power in Egypt would thus make Gamal Mubarak an illegitimate ruler (El Said, interview, 2004; Nafa, interview, 2004). For such reasons the succession process was resisted by the old guard, who saw it as contradicting a fundamental principle of Islamic governance. It was clear that overall, ideological dichotomy or not, the MB opposed the succession process, and this was made clear by the movement's senior leaders, whether of the old guard or the new generation. The MB's supreme leader, Mohammed Akef, at a post-fast meal in Cairo during Ramadan in 2005, stated: 'We categorically reject inheritance of rule in any form. We believe the constitutional amendment aims to enshrine inheritance, but God willing this won't happen and we will fight it relentlessly' (*Haaretz*, 13 October 2005).

Akef also declared that his movement rejected the notion of, specifically, Gamal Mubarak 'inheriting' power. In an important statement in May 2006, the MB highlighted Gamal's elitist image, saying that the younger Mubarak 'has nothing to do with the people and knows nothing about the people' (Shehata, 2006). Former Deputy Supreme Guide Mohammad Habib, a representative of the new generation of leaders, consistently made similar remarks. The voice of the MB was strengthened by its success in the 2005 parliamentary elections, when it acquired 88 seats; this provided it with a large bloc in parliament, which in turn allowed it to raise its voice in opposition to Gamal Mubarak taking over from his father. Despite the political platform which the MB constructed in the world of Egyptian politics, the degree of its impact depended on three factors: its willingness to join hands with alternative opposition actors; its ability to mobilise its social base; and its readiness to enter a new phase of resistance to the state, through street protests and demonstrations (El Said, interview, 2004). The evidence indicated that the MB was willing to do all the above to exert influence on the political succession process, making life as difficult as possible for the government which aimed to push that process through with the minimum noise possible.

The MB thus used its position in the Egyptian parliament and syndicates – particularly that of the lawyers – to criticise and oppose the succession process, and in joining this opposition the professional class was further politicised (El Said, interview, 2004). However, the MB was aware of the fact that the strength of its influence also depended on its ability to create a new sphere of opposition to the Egyptian state. This resulted in its going beyond voicing criticism via parliament and the syndicates to involvement in political dissent through a series of street protests and demonstrations. This dynamism of the MB heightened the government's fear of opposition to its succession plans developing both inside and outside the political system, in particular its fear of an MB-led popular movement. The MB, along with other social forces such as the 20 March Movement for Change, the outlawed Communist Party, the would-be Al-Karama Movement Party and the Hisham Mubarak Law Centre (HMLC), launched a Popular Movement for Change with the slogan 'no to renewal, no to hereditary succession, yes to electing the president of the republic' (*Al Ahram*, 23–29 June 2005). This represented the first oppositional alliance against the politics of succession, and its impact was significant in galvanising the public, building public awareness and raising opposition to the inheritance of power in Egypt. The MB also participated regularly with *Kefayah*, in holding anti-succession demonstrations, and was involved in the first-ever anti-Gamal Mubarak demonstration in December 2004. This was the more significant since it was held in the run-up to the presidential and parliamentary elections in 2005. In March of that year the MB took to the streets, with a number of demonstrations in the various districts of Cairo; the objective was to demand political reform, and once again to protest at the inheritance of power (*Al Ahram*, 23–29 June 2005). Two months later the MB held a number of pro-reform protests in Cairo and in other towns in Egypt. This regular taking to the streets by the MB, its mobilisation of the Egyptian public and its willingness to cross ideological lines by embracing the *Kefayah* movement and the communist party indicated the MB's desire to put as much pressure as possible on the Egyptian government leading up to the 2005 elections. The hope was to force political reform and to obstruct the managed process of political succession (*Al Ahram*, 16–22 September 2004).

This pursuance of a cycle of political dissent through regular street demonstrations was a new addition to the MB's portfolio in its struggle with the government, and the movement's growing influence on the succession process created a dangerous situation for the government, which, in response, began to take measures to limit the political space for mobilisation, mounting a major offensive against the MB and any other political actors viewed as being vocally against the succession process. After the 2005 elections the State of Emergency Law was renewed and municipal elections were suspended for two years. The MB made it clear that this was to be seen as the state's attempt to limit the movement's influence and thus to facilitate the succession process. Mohammed Habib stated: 'I see the main goal of delaying the elections by two years as laying the foundations for the inheritance of power and opening the door wide open for Gamal Mubarak to be the candidate for the presidency.' He added: 'There is a view that during these two years it is possible to put Gamal Mubarak forward as a candidate. There was a step taken with his appointment as an assistant Secretary General in the NDP' (*The Daily Star*, June 2006).

At the same time the government began a major security offensive against the MB, a large number of whose activists were arrested by the police and security forces. It is important to note that despite its draconian policy towards the MB the government had, to some degree, been dealing with the movement in a different manner compared to the 1990s. This time MB activists were arrested during daylight, in restaurants and coffee houses or while picking up children from school; and this new tactic of the Egyptian state – to hit the MB whenever and wherever it could – of course led to a deterioration in its relations with the movement. The offensive was directed in particular at the new generation of pragmatic activists, those who had been instrumental in changing the character of the MB, and had been the face of its opposition to the succession process. Thus such individuals as Essam El Eyrian, Ibrahim El Zafrani, Kharait El-Shater, Mohammed Morsi and Hassan al Hayawan had all been detained since the 2005 elections. Kharait El-Shater, a key figure in the movement, was given a five-year prison sentence – an indication of the government's efforts to disable the pragmatic wing of the movement. There is no doubt that this constituted a strategic effort by the Egyptian state to damage the MB and thus to weaken its impact on the political succession.

The intense level of political oppression in the years that followed the 2005 elections, led the MB to predict that President Mubarak, was planning to transfer power to Gamal soon. Speaking in 2006, Mohammed Habib stated: 'The matter will not go on for more than a year.' The MB expected an increase in restrictions on democracy and free speech, and the arrest of thousands of the regime's political opponents, in order to enable Gamal to become the new ruler of Egypt. Habib went on to say:

> The government or the regime is trying to send a message to the brotherhood so that they reduce their activities, tone down their statements ... This requires more restrictions, persecutions, jailings and perhaps military tribunals, so that the atmosphere is prepared and the stage is set for the inheritance of the scenario. (*The Daily Star*, June 2006)

The MB entered a new phase in its struggle with the Egyptian government and this had an impact on opinion in the MB – in particular as to whether it was in the best interests of the movement to continue with the political dissent which led to it facing a new wave of government oppression.

The clampdown on the MB in response to its growing political weight and its anti-Gamal position led to a divergence of opinion within the movement regarding its policy towards the succession process. Mohammed Akef and the old guard saw a need for the MB to continue with its campaign of dissent – otherwise its ideology (i.e. the Islamic legitimacy of the country's ruler) would be sacrificed, and it would lose credibility among its social base. However, the pragmatic new generation, which bore the brunt of the clampdown, began to show signs of a different opinion, believing that to focus primarily on the succession process would affect the MB's long-term interests in Egypt, such as political reform and its own legal status (Altman, 2006). Instead, they believed that the movement should change its stance, and exploit the government's difficulty in securing a smooth succession by seeking to end the State of Emergency and to change Article 76 of the constitution. This toned-down posture was advocated by a leading new-generation activist, Mohammed Al Shatir, a member of the MB parliamentary bloc, and there was even talk, in particular from the new-generation leadership (which after all represents the movement's political face), that the MB might strike a deal with the government. There was indeed evidence to indicate that members of Gamal's Policy Secretariat met with new-generation MB leaders seeking to secure the movement's neutrality and its withdrawal from opposition activities against the succession process, although this was denied by the movement itself (Altman, 2006). Given this development, Muntasar al Zayyat, a lawyer and leading expert on Islamist movements, suggested that the MB would covertly cooperate with the government to help it achieve Gamal's succession (Altman, 2006). The government was aware of the ideological divergence in the MB between the old orthodox and the pragmatic new groupings, and this provided it with an opportunity to try to co-opt the movement, in particular the new-generation leadership, and thereby to defuse its opposition to the succession process. The government's violence towards the new-generation activists led the latter to change their views on the succession process, moving closer to the state's position in order to secure the MB's interests. The government saw these activists as more prepared to play by the rules of its game, and was therefore willing to hold discussions with them, but remained concerned at the position taken by the MB's old guard, who were less eager to cooperate with the state. However, the division in the MB did indeed provide the government with the opportunity to manipulate the MB in order to weaken it and neutralise its opposition to the succession process, which if successful would have removed a major obstacle to the transference of power from Hosni to Gamal Mubarak.

Overall, it is apparent that the MB had an influence on the succession process, which allowed it to demonstrate once again its political weight in Egypt. This led to the state apparatus resorting to its usual policy of oppression towards the MB, but this failed to undermine or even seriously weaken it. At the same time, the government realised the danger of adopting an oppressive policy towards the MB, given the implications for the future stability and survival of the regime, and was forced into private meetings with the movement to secure its support and to neutralise it. This was facilitated by the MB new-generation leadership's changing views on the succession process and on entertaining discussions with the government. If the MB's opposition was indeed neutralised, a key social and political obstacle would have been removed, and the succession bid of Gamal Mubarak would become much more likely to succeed. In any event, the political weight of the MB, and particularly of its new generation of activist leaders, was finally acknowledged by the Egyptian government in its attempts at reconciliation with and pacification of the movement.

Conclusion

This chapter has explored the process of political succession in Egypt, taking into consideration the actors involved, the process of grooming and the forces driving that process. In addition to this the role of political actors such as the military and the MB has been explored in terms of their influence on the politics of succession. Both these actors had an influence and both were a source of concern to the government. In order to deal with military officials the government had to adopt a policy of courting them to win their confidence in the succession process, and also relied on support from the US, which approved of Gamal's succession bid. Although the military had reservations over Gamal, it seemed likely this would be overcome by US influence and the appointment of a Vice-President from within the officer ranks, or at least from among those with close links to the military. On the other hand, dealing with the MB was made much more difficult for the government by the political clout the movement wielded in the country. Despite the government's oppression, it was not able to neutralise the MB's power, and this pushed it into pursuing a policy of negotiating with the movement to secure the succession of Gamal Mubarak. The MB's new-generation leadership seemed likely to discuss and then accept concessions made by the government, so as win benefits for the future – thus clearing the way for the succession of Gamal Mubarak.

8

CONTINUITY AND DISCONTINUITY: ELECTORAL PROMISES, LIBERALISATION AND OPPOSITION POLITICS

This chapter will begin by exploring the course of economic and political change in Egypt in the context of the succession process, in particular the level of continuity and discontinuity. By looking at the electoral promises made by Hosni Mubarak in the 2005 presidential elections, the programme of Gamal Mubarak and his relations with the MB, this will give an understanding of the level of continuity between father and son and the implications of this for reform in Egypt.

Mubarak's electoral promises: economic and political transformation, or stagnation?

Given wide-ranging socio-economic and political demands in Egypt, it was only natural for promises of economic and political reform to feature prominently in Hosni Mubarak's presidential campaign in September 2005 (*Al Ahram*, 4–10August 2005; *The Arabist*, 26 August 2005). Mubarak set out his reform agenda in a speech he made in Menoufiya, his home town, on 28 July 2005.

The following three excerpts from his speech indicate his emphasis on economic and political reforms:

> Together we will work towards greater democratisation, liberating our economy in such a way as to protect the interests of peasants and workers and with an eye on the welfare of the economically disadvantaged.

> The emergency laws have aided us in our fight against terrorism. Indeed, a great many nations are now enacting comprehensive anti-terrorist legislation. The time has come for us, too, within the next period to formulate legislation capable of undermining and uprooting terrorism so our nation can be spared the evils terror brings. We are [aiming] for an anti-terror law that can provide a legislative substitute for the emergency laws.

> I promise to work towards implementing economic and social policies that will increase job opportunities, improve living standards, guarantee decent conditions for the retired and allow the state to improve public education, health care, housing and transport. Together we will build a tomorrow where the middle class can strive for better living standards, where the disadvantaged have adequate social security provision and where the rights of women receive the attention they deserve. (*Al Ahram*, 4–10 August 2005)

Though Mubarak placed strong emphasis on economic and political reforms during the 2005 campaign, he later began to shift the primary focus onto popular economic issues such as poverty and unemployment. This was in comparison to his presidential rivals, Ayman Nour of *al Ghad* and Nouman Gomma of *al Wafd* party, both of whom focused on political reforms connected to the lifting of the state of emergency, the removal of restrictions on political parties and the expansion of civil political freedoms (*Open Democracy*, 30 August 2005; *VoaNews*, 17 August 2005; *The Economist*, 25 August 2005). Mubarak pledged to carry out economic policies designed to promote industry, to tackle employment (proposing a programme to create 4.5 million jobs for young people in the coming six years), and to encourage exports of farm produce and to boost the competitiveness of the country's agriculture. He described farmers as the main pillar of Egyptian society, noting that any plans for future development could not be implemented without the involvement of farmers and the agricultural sector. In addition Mubarak outlined his commitment to improving the salaries of 5.2 million civil servants and to doubling the number of families receiving social-security benefits, from 650,000 to 1.3 million (*English People's Daily*, 24 August 2005). Economic reforms became a cornerstone of his presidential bid, but his proposals came under criticism: question marks hung over the feasibility of the economic policies he had outlined – there was a feeling that populist economic rhetoric underlay Mubarak's speeches and pledges rather than a firm belief in being able to deliver on what he was promising.

While economic growth for the fiscal year 2004–05 soared to a record five per cent and most other economic indicators were on the rise, the economic measures promised by Mubarak were criticised as requiring the slashing of subsidies and the raising of public debt, risking skyrocketing inflation. As a result Mubarak's economic promises were quickly dismissed as unrealistic by some of his election rivals. 'Why hasn't Mubarak created all these jobs during the 24 years he has already spent in power?' asked *al Wafd* party leader Nouman Gomma (*Iran Daily*, 4 September 2005). Several analysts also pointed out that the ultra-liberal policies pushed by Mubarak's son Gamal were hardly compatible with the social commitments of the former's presidential campaign. Ahmad Nagger, an Egyptian economist, stated: 'The job creation programme is simply not realistic. In

24 years, 291,000 jobs were created every year. How can we expect to see this figure double in only six years?' (*Iran Daily*, 4 September 2005). The WB also estimated in 2006 that unemployment in Egypt was running at around 20 per cent, a figure that would make it difficult for Nazif's government to fulfil Hosni Mubarak's election promise to create 4.5 million jobs in the following six years (*Al Ahram*, 16–22 March 2006). Nor was the WB optimistic about the chances of achieving other economic targets, pointing out that:

The deficit in the trade balance grew last year to more than $7 billion, with imports increasing by 30 per cent annually. Balancing the budget and reducing public indebtedness were urgent requirements, while the budget deficit had skyrocketed from 0.6 per cent of GDP in 1996/1997 to 9 per cent in 2005/2006, and public debts now stood at more than 60 per cent of GDP. (*Al Ahram*, 16–22 March 2006).

Or as, Nabil Abdel-Fattah of the Al-Ahram Center for Political and Strategic Studies put it:

What is clear at this point is that the NDP has shown itself to be lacking both the imagination and the will to address the fundamental problems besetting Egypt's political and economic life. While it has referred to some of the chronic problems Egypt faces during its campaign it has failed to acknowledge that these very problems are a result of the failed policies of the past 24 years. (*Al Ahram*, 25–31 August 2005)

The campaign, moreover, failed to tackle what many argue was chronic corruption plaguing Egypt's economic performance. As *al Tagammu* MP Abul-Ezz Al-Hariri said:

In his campaign pledges the NDP candidate has not once referred to the corruption which has become a mode of governance. Nor is it clear how he can pledge to establish 1,000 factories over a six-year period when the government's understanding of economic reform seems not to extend beyond privatising the public sector. (*Al Ahram*, 25–31 August 2005)

Criticism of Mubarak's economic pledges was clear, with concerns about an economic and social crisis stemming from the economic reforms he promised. Mubarak was further criticised when the new cabinet was introduced after the parliamentary elections in November 2005: its membership pointed in the direction of the government's economic reforms, which raised further concerns about future socio-economic conditions in the country.

In this new cabinet the number of ministers with business connections rose to six, leading the opposition press to charge that Prime Minister Nazif's cabinet looked more like the executive board of a private company (*Al Ahram*, 29 December–4 January 2006). For example, prominent businessman Mohamed Mansour, the new Transportation Minister, was a former president of the American Chamber of Commerce in Egypt. Ali El-Moselhi, who headed the new Social Solidarity Ministry, also came from a private-sector background, though most recently had been the head of the Egyptian postal service and had implemented a wide-ranging modernisation project.

In reply to growing concerns about the increasing role of businessmen in the cabinet, Nazif argued that the inclusion of pragmatic and business-minded ministers had boosted the government's financial and economic progress; the concept of businessmen becoming cabinet ministers should no longer be seen as a bad thing – 'Businessmen have the privilege of mixing administrative experience with a forward-looking and global mentality.' To support his argument Nazif highlighted the rise in GDP from LE485 to LE537 billion ($93 billion), the vast increase in foreign exchange reserves, from $14.8 to $22 billion, the fall in external debt, from $30 to $28.9 billion, and the drop in inflation from 16.7 per cent of GDP to 3.1 per cent – all of which he argued had taken place in one year (*Al Ahram*, 2–8 February 2006). This attempt to deal with the concerns of the political opposition seemed unconvincing, as the cabinet's key economic portfolios remained in the same hands, indicating that the government would continue to pursue the same liberal economic policies witnessed in Nazif's first term. These policies did not win the confidence of the public – the cutting of subsidies and the pursuance of privatisation were two areas in which Nazif's cabinet faced its harshest opposition since July 2004. Critics argued that he was merely following the orders of the IFIs, which were pushing for the liberalisation and globalisation of the Egyptian economy. It was to aid this process, critics argued, that ministers with a private-sector background were drafted into the new cabinet. The pursuance of liberalisation and privatisation, given their probable consequences – unemployment, inflation and the cutting of subsidies – seemed to indicate a lack of commitment by the cabinet and Hosni Mubarak to social development. Socio-economic improvements seemed unlikely if the government continued with the same economic strategy it had implemented in the past. The Egyptian people's experience of liberal economic policies had not been good, and it was unlikely that policies of this nature would bring a drastic change in daily life.

It looked as though the government's political strategy would be determined by the extent of the socio-economic crisis and the challenges it faced from political actors such as the MB. Mubarak's pledges of political reform and change therefore carried little weight with the political opposition and the Egyptian people, given that promises of this nature have been made in the past, as in his 1999 presidential referendum. Mubarak's agenda in 1999 included economic as well as political pledges, such as promises of constitutional reform stimulating political-party activity, bringing new and more youthful elements into leadership positions, developing the electoral system, deregulating the media, supporting the rule of law, fighting corruption and enhancing the freedom of civil-society institutions (*Al Ahram*, 30 September–6 October 1999; International Crisis Group, 30 September 2003). In an address to university students in Alexandria on 25 August 1999, Mubarak stated that the NDP must work 'to effect that change or reform that will enrich the process of popular participation in public life in a manner that will not prejudice the nation's higher interests.' He also emphasised that Egypt's revival did not depend on the government's efforts alone. Rather, 'it must be borne collectively by the institutions of government and the organisations of civil society, from the political parties to the syndicates, unions and community associations' (*Al Ahram*, 30 September–6 October, 1999).

Despite these pledges, little progress in political reform was made by Mubarak after 1999, with the NDP continuing its hegemony over society. Cosmetic changes were introduced, providing a veneer of reform but doing little to strengthen political life in Egypt. The political changes were piecemeal, introduced to deal with growing internal pressure and to create the context for the politics of succession rather than to facilitate reform. The real political issues, such as constitutional reform, the independence of the judiciary, separation of powers and the empowerment of civil society, did not enter the mindset of the Egyptian government. Given the hollow pledges made in 1999, the 2005 versions could be seen as an old story repeating itself, especially if one takes into consideration the composition of the new cabinet, the liberal economic strategy, the role of the MB and the process of political succession. The process of economic change thus seemed likely to be consistent with past policy, with the regimes survival dictating political strategy, in particular taking into consideration the succession process and the political clout of the MB. This can be seen from the process of political de-liberalisation witnessed in Egypt after the 2005 elections.

After Mubarak's re-election for a fifth six-year term in office, in September 2005, the Egyptian government went back on promises of political reform and introduced further restrictions. This strategy should be understood in the context of the politics of succession and the challenge of the MB. For example, to contain the MB the government postponed local elections, scheduled to take place in Spring 2006, for two years (*Al Ahram*, 16–22 February 2006). This meant that the possibility was removed of the MB acquiring the 250 seats required for it to contest the presidential elections set for 2011 (*The Mercury News*, 29 April 2006; *The Arabist*, 19 June 2006). Also, in December 2005 the leader of the opposition *al Ghad* party, Ayman Nour, was jailed for five years on forgery charges. Nour claimed the charges were false, and he was being punished for challenging Hosni Mubarak and criticising his son Gamal (*Daily Times*, 25 December 2005; *www.arabnews*, 25 December 2005). In the context of the political succession, the Egyptian state had thus pre-empted two obstacles to the transition of power, by the postponement of the local elections and the jailing of Ayman Nour.

To the same end, the government used its coercive arm, after the 2005 election, to weaken the judicial reform movement in Egypt, which it viewed as a possible hindrance to the succession process. In February 2006 the Supreme Judicial Council stripped four pro-reform judges of their judicial immunity, to allow State Security prosecutors to question them. The government then charged these four – Hisham al-Bastawisi, Mahmoud Makki, his brother Ahmad Makki and Mahmoud al-Khodairi, president of the Alexandria Judges' Club – with 'defaming the state' (*Ikhwanweb*, 4 May 2006). Two of them, Mahmoud Makki and al-Bastawisi, were summoned to a disciplinary board for alleging that certain judges from within the judiciary helped rig the previous year's parliamentary polls, which had seen the ruling party retain a firm grip on power (*BBC News*, 18 April; 20 April; 24 April 2006). The judge's syndicate had become one of the most potent symbols of the drive for reform in Egypt over the previous year; Amr Hamzawy, of the Carnegie Endowment for International Peace, said the regime's message was clear: 'It's a lesson to everyone who dares to cross the red lines,' said the Washington-based analyst (*Middle East Online*, 20 April 2006).

Human-rights organisations expressed grave concern about a police attack against peaceful demonstrators outside the Judges' Club in the early hours of Monday 1 May 2006. An eyewitness told Human Rights Watch that a large number of men, apparently plainclothes police, launched an attack on some 40 people who had been holding a round-the-clock vigil in support of the two judges threatened with dismissal. They beat 15 of the demonstrators, and Judge Mahmud Abd al-Latif Hamza as he emerged from the club (*Ikhwanweb*, 4 May; *The Daily Star*, 27 April; *Al Ahram*, 27 April–3 May 2006). Twelve of the demonstrators were detained for 15 days, for investigation on charges of destroying public property.

The oppressive attitude of the government towards the pro-reform judges shows the importance it attached to controlling state institutions and to securing the succession in Egypt (*Middle East Online*, 20 April 2006). The judiciary continued with its challenge, contributing to the demand for political change, while the Egyptian state continued to resist any such demands – it extended the state of emergency by another two years, furthering the country's slide into deeper authoritarianism. The government justified this extension as a response to the terrorist attacks on the holiday resort of Dahab in April 2006 (*Ikhwanweb*, 2 May; 30 April; Reuters, 30 April 2006). The state of emergency failed to boost security, however, as the country since experienced a number of other terrorist attacks; it was simply used by the government to restrict political activism that could threaten the state's powers and structures.

President Mubarak's economic and political reform agenda seemed to have been derailed before it had even begun. The experience of the 1990s was one of political de-liberalisation at a time of socio-economic crisis and liberal economic reform, and this became the reality of Egypt. On the political level, there was an increase in political de-liberalisation, especially after the brief openings before the presidential and parliamentary elections in 2005 (*Ikhwanweb*, 12 May 2006). President Mubarak's economic pledges were criticised as ill thought-out and generally unfeasible given the severity of the country's problems. Also, the nature of the new cabinet inspired little confidence that it would be able to deliver on socio-economic commitments, such as decreasing the level of poverty and creating employment. Thus the continuance of Hosni Mubarak's economic and political strategy did not bode well for the future of economic and political change in Egypt; and this raised the question of the political succession, in particular whether a shift in economic and political strategy could be expected under Gamal.

The political succession: economic and political implications

After the 2005 elections, Gamal Mubarak and his close associates moved into key political positions. Gamal himself rose in the hierarchy of the governing NDP, being named as one of three NDP deputy secretaries-general, and 20 of his associates took other high-ranking posts in the party. Ahmed Ezz, a steel magnate and close associate of Gamal, was also appointed to the NDP secretariat in the reshuffle. Gamal and his supporters displaced some (though not all) of the veteran NDP activists, and political observers saw in these moves a gradual shift toward putting the NDP at the service of the president's son (*allbusiness.com*, 23 January 2006; *Egypt Today*, March 2006). As a result of all these political developments after the 2005 elections, the succession process proceeded rapidly, and questions arose as to the level of continuity or discontinuity in economic and political reform to be expected under Gamal, as compared to his father.

A political succession process would seem to indicate an internal political change, but this was unlikely to have a substantial bearing on the Egyptian state, in particular its autocratic structures and mechanisms; it would simply buttress the present political hierarchy, but with a younger face at the apex. Gamal's succession seemed likely to result in a reshuffle in the political elite, bringing into the limelight more like-minded individuals who shared his economic and political vision for Egypt. However, Gamal's rapid elevation in the NDP was only with the consent of the party's political power brokers, and therefore despite any reshuffle of the political elite he would inevitably remain dependent on certain political elements for continuing support and advice (El Said, interview, 2004; Nafa, interview 2004; el Abdel Fattah, interview, 2004). This dependency would no doubt restrict Gamal's political vision to that approved by those on whom he relied and from whom he sought support. Despite the obvious impediment to political reform which this dependency would mean, it would give Gamal much-needed political support among the Egyptian political elite, who would fight his corner when he wanted to make an economic or political change. However, this would depend in turn on Gamal's management skills, in particular the extent to which he was able to balance the different key competing political actors and institutions effectively, without being seen to prioritise or favour one over the other – which could lead to political conflict. Such management of the political elite and institutions is not easy, as the tenure of Basher al Assad in Syria has clearly demonstrated: he has faced constant problems in dealing with the Syrian political elite and related state organs (Zisser, 2000; 2003; 2004; Gambill, 2000; 2003; Leverett, 2005). This has weakened his leadership, and the Baath state in Syria. If Gamal could not manage and balance the political elite and state organs in a shrewd and careful manner, a similar situation to that in Syria could emerge, throwing Egypt into political paralysis as a result of intra-regime and inter-elite conflict (El Said, interview, 2004; el Abdel Fattah, interview, 2004).

There was no doubt that various strata of the political elite would resist any reform that put their interests at risk, but despite this obvious dilemma for Gamal Mubarak, a question hung over the extent to which he and his liberal associates were driven by a strong desire to implement bold political reforms and to meet the political elite head on when it resisted change. The pro-Gamalists in the Egyptian cabinet focused on pursuing a liberal economic strategy involving liberalisation and privatisation, and this, rather than talk of political reform, informed their discourse. It seemed that Gamal's presidency would be dominated more by an economic than a political agenda, given his belief that economic change is central to political development. It was thus unlikely there would be a substantial drive by him and his associates to introduce bold political reforms. To exemplify this point, the rise of liberals in Jordanian politics has been significant since King Abdullah took over in 1999, and this resulted in a discourse centring on economic liberalisation, with discussions on political reform effectively marginalised. There has been increasing centralisation of political power in the hands of King Abdullah, resulting in liberal politicians being referred to as 'liberal authoritarians' (Ryan, 2005; Schwedler, 2002). Meanwhile, the status of the Jordanian security forces increased, leaving no doubt that the role even of liberal politicians is set by the Jordanian monarchy.

Therefore Gamal's leadership looked set to focus on an economic strategy centring on economic liberalisation, privatisation and the opening-up of Egypt to regional and international capital markets (*Democracy Digest*, 23 July 2004). There was concern that the capitalist class would benefit excessively from such reforms, and that the destructive nature of the market forces they would unleash would damage the interests of the people. Gamal's economic strategy could bring about social legitimacy if the economic reforms delivered, and improved the economic position of the Egyptian masses (Cunningham, 2005). There was talk of revitalisation in the economy, as a result of the economic reforms already introduced by Gamal and his associates, but the question remained as to the extent to which economic growth would benefit the man in the street; there seemed to be no change, for example, in the levels of unemployment and poverty. If Mubarak's election economic pledges, to create four million jobs in six years and to raise living standards, were not fulfilled by the Egyptian state, economists predicted a worsening of the socio-economic situation in the short term (*Al Ahram*, 25–31 August 2005). If the wide-ranging promises made by Gamal lead to no material results, a gap of trust would develop between him and the Egyptian people.

The previous Prime Minister, Atif Obeid, suffered from an immense lack of public trust for the failure of his government to deliver improvements in the lives of ordinary Egyptians. Promises were made and economic successes announced by Obeid, but the latter were not experienced by the ordinary Egyptian. Thus Gamal's expected economic strategy, could have had positive or negative consequences depending on the manner in which his economic reforms were handled. The outcome of such reforms and how their benefits were actually distributed to the people would have had a decisive impact on the public support-base for a Gamal regime. A wide support-base was crucial for Gamal to deal with potential problems stemming from economic and political failure. A movement in the political orientation and position of the NDP was a possible way of broadening its support base, not an easy strategy however, as a number of problems emerged.

Gamal Mubarak and the orientation of the National Democratic Party

The centre ground in Egyptian politics has traditionally been held by the NDP, but with the ascendancy of Gamal there was talk of the party possibly moving to strengthen its social roots and widen its support base (El Said, interview, 2004). The problem with this was that the party was riven by a number of political schisms which characterised Egyptian politics since the 1952 revolution (International Crisis Group, 4 October 2005). Schisms had been factors in Egyptian politics for some time, and a movement in the NDP would be difficult to engineer since it would necessitate building a new coalition, with alternative political actors. This was extremely difficult to envisage, given that the political coalition embedded in state structures (i.e. the old guard of politicians, the military and the security services) would not wish to adopt a new political position which could damage their economic and/or political interests.

Also, any effort to build a coalition with Islamic partners, such as the MB, would bring accusations of the NDP exploiting religion for political ends: exactly the accusations the NDP itself directed at the MB. As discussed above, Gamal Mubarak would remain dependent on certain existing political elements in the Egyptian hierarchy, and this would make it even more difficult for him to change the composition of the existing coalition to open up a path for change in the NDP's positioning (el Abdel Fattah, interview, 2004; El Said, interview, 2004). Also, the political opposition would not view a movement by the NDP away from the centre too favourably, as this would indicate the party moving into the opposition's territory, further damaging a position already significantly harmed by internal disputes, rivalry and corruption. Therefore Gamal would no doubt have to take into consideration relations with political actors both inside and outside the political elite. Though relations with internal actors matter for the survival of any future Gamal government, it is important not to neglect outside actors, in particular the US.

Egypt–US relations under Gamal Mubarak

In order to ensure political stability Gamal would have to take into consideration numerous relationships, such as those with the business community, the political elite, the security services, the military and the political opposition. An international relationship providing Gamal with important support would be that with Washington; this was important to Egypt under Hosni Mubarak and was likely to remain a central fixture of Egypt's foreign policy. It was thought that Gamal's presidential candidacy was backed by Washington, and this seemed important at a time when American hegemony was stronger than ever in the Middle East, and when the US was pushing for change in the region – although the extent of political change desired by the US is debatable, even with the election of President Barack Obama. For Egypt, as an important strategic state for the US, this backing of Gamal by Washington carried further weight and importance, as the US only supported those they could trust in the presidential hot seat in Egypt (Nafa, interview, 2004; El Said, interview, 2004).

As emphasised previously, the military plays a key role in Egyptian politics; this was well understood by the US, and there was thus no doubt that the US would need its approval before helping to ensure the transition of Gamal to power. The relationship would provide much-needed support for Gamal, but could also backfire given his closeness to the US administration. His father, on becoming president, decided to pursue a populist foreign policy to build his own legitimacy, which included public distancing from the US to appease the strong anti-US sentiments among the Egyptian masses (Al-Awadi, 2004). This political manoeuvre was an option for Gamal, who was already viewed publicly as being liberal-minded and pro-American. The war in Iraq, the backing of the US for Israeli military action in Lebanon and its threatening position towards Syria and Iran heightened the levels of anti-Americanism in the Middle East; therefore a close relationship with the US could undermine Gamal's search for legitimacy among the Egyptian people.

However, the election of President Obama looked more positive for Gamal, with respect in particular to the former's desire to improve the image of the US in the Middle East and his talk of engaging Iran and Syria. Regardless of whether President Obama was successful, the support of the US would give Gamal Mubarak would be crucial in his succession bid, as the process was beset by dilemmas and challenges, particularly from internal political actors such as the MB. This led to the Egyptian government attempting to neutralise the movement (see Chapter 7). Given the fact that the MB is a key political actor in Egypt, the position taken by the Egyptian government towards the MB after the 2005 elections must be taken into consideration, in particular as to whether there had been any change in that position and in the prospective approach of Gamal Mubarak toward the MB.

Gamal Mubarak, the MB and implications for the future process of political reform in Egypt

The position of the Egyptian government and of the NDP remained unchanged with regard to providing the MB with a legal platform in Egyptian politics. However, despite this rigid position a statement made by Kamal El-Shazli, a leading member of the old guard within the NDP, to the London-based *Al Hayat* newspaper (30 October 2005), reflected a slight change in the Egyptian government position. He stated: 'The Muslim Brotherhood has established a prominent presence on the political scene ... they have their supporters.' This was the first time a senior government official publicly acknowledged the MB's influence and role in Egyptian politics. El-Shazli continued: 'We have ourselves developed as a ruling party and as a government and things have changed. The Brotherhood has a street presence and wants to engage in political work. We don't mind' (*Al Ahram*, 10–16 November 2005).

Clear signs of a policy shift by the NDP towards the MB was seen during the 2005 parliamentary election campaign. The MB was allowed to use their traditional slogan, 'Islam is the Solution', in the constituencies they contested, and their candidates were allowed to present themselves as '*Ikhwan*' ('brotherhood') candidates, which in the past had not been permitted. In general, the MB this time was allowed actively to engage in society, without intimidation and harassment – a decided shift in state policy. However, despite this change the NDP still saw no contradiction in recognising and acknowledging the MB's influence and political role in society, while at the same time denying its legitimacy as a political party. In the same interview with *Al Hayat*, El-Shazli suggested: 'If they want to engage in politics as the MB then they are free to do so. A political party though was not an option' (*Al Ahram*, 10–16 November 2005). In reality the Egyptian government was not ceding new ground to the MB, baulking at the crucial question of legality, which the MB had been seeking for the past 25 years.

While the politics of succession loomed in Egypt indications did not provide a positive picture with respect to Gamal Mubarak's attitude towards the MB. He called for 'illegal' parties to be banned from participating in formal politics, and although he did not refer directly to the MB it was clear in an interview with *Al Jazeera* (25 January 2006) where he was directing his comments. In May 2006 there was some strong rhetoric from the government about barring individual MB candidates from future elections. Pro-Gamalist Prime Minister Ahmed Nazif described the MB members of parliament as a 'secret cell', threatening that he would 'not allow them to form a parliamentary bloc in the future nor to assume any role in the political arena' (*Al Mesryoon*, 30 May 2006). In addition to Nazif's statement there was severe criticism from other government officials, including Mufid Shihab, Minister for Parliamentary Affairs, Hatim Al Gabali, Minister of Health, and Ahmed Darwish, Minister for Administrative Development. These criticisms were in line with the government's and Gamal's firm stance against the MB after the 2005 parliamentary elections. Nazif went further, by suggesting ways in which the government could reduce the MB's representation in future parliaments: one of his proposals was to introduce an electoral system which combines voting for individuals and voting for party lists, though this would require constitutional change. 'If we amended the constitution to allow that, then we could obtain better representation for the parties in parliament, even if so far I don't know whether that would happen or not,' Nazif told the independent newspaper *Al Masry Al Youm* (*Arab Online*, 1 June 2006); in answer to a question on how the Egyptian government might put into practice his wish to prevent the MB from forming a bloc in the next parliament.

However, some elements of the NDP's reformist wing seemed to recognise that if they did not allow the opposition parties enough manoeuvring room in society, they would be forced to legalise the MB. Even Gamal's political advisor Mohammed Kamal stated in an interview with the International Crisis Group:

> In the future, definitely, the issue of the relation of religion with the state will have to be resolved. There is a definite need to integrate [the Brotherhood] into the political system. Personally, I am against legalising them as a political party. I think the solution is to enhance and strengthen the secular political parties in order to fill the vacuum in the political system that is being filled by the Islamists. (4 October 2005, p. 28).

However, there was no guarantee that a strong political alternative to the NDP would emerge in Egypt, as a direct result of vested interests in the party which were resistant to the process of political change. Neither the government, nor Gamal Mubarak, nor the NDP appeared to have adopted a positive position on providing legal space for the MB, and this remained a stumbling block in the movement's quest for legitimacy. Gamal's position with respect to the MB was something the government found difficult to maintain, given the pressure created by Egyptian, British and US commentary on the process of political reform, and given the changing attitudes of the political opposition toward the MB in Egypt (*Al Ahram*, 15–21 December 2005; Hamzawy and Brown, 2005; *Al Jazeera*, 22 June 2005).

In response to the MB's growing political weight, and to its participation in Egyptian political life through its involvement in parliament and professional syndicates, the political opposition changed its perceptions of and attitudes towards the MB. Newcomers to the Egyptian political scene such as the *Kefayah* movement and *al Ghad* party adopted clear positions in relation to the movement. Ayman Nour told the International Crisis Group: 'We respect them and the fact that they have been a political current for nearly 80 years now. We are in favour of them being legal' (International Crisis Group, interview, 4 October 2005, p. 25). That *al Ghad* recognised the MB as a political actor in Egyptian society can be further seen in Ayman Nour's meeting with the MB leadership in the run-up to the 2005 presidential elections, held to gain the MB's support for his candidacy. George Ishak of *Kefayah* has commented:

> I appreciate that they will be a political party; let them show themselves. I believe that if they were able to compete in an election, they would win 10 to 15 per cent. But for as long as they are forced to remain in hiding, people think there are three or four million of them; this is not true; there are 30,000 to 40,000 of them, no more. (International Crisis Group, interview, 4 October 2005, p. 25)

Older parties in Egypt, such as *al Nasseriyya* and *al Tagammu*, were more ambivalent towards the MB, but nevertheless their position changed. *Al Nasseriyya* favoured involving the MB and the Islamists in the political process, and supported a legal party for them. On the other hand *al Tagammu* was split. Rifat al Saeed, for example, was a member well known for his opposition in general to the Islamist trend within Egypt and in particular to the MB; his opposition to political Islam marks much of his academic and scholarly output. He devotes a weekly column in *Al-Ahali*, under the title 'A page from Egypt's history', to debunking the MB's role in Egyptian society. He coined the term *'muta'aslimin'*, which carries a multitude of negative connotations, including the cynical use of religion to attain political power (*Al Ahram*, 7–13 July 2005). However, al Saeed's views were not consistently held throughout *al Tagammu* party, with other members more receptive to the MB and its quest for legitimacy: they advocated the movement's development into a *hizb madani* ('civil party') with an Islamic background (Kish, interview, 2004). *Al Wafd*, the oldest liberal party in Egypt, took the position that it would work and cooperate with the MB. For example, the party's former leader, Nouman Gomma, visited the MB prior to the 2005 presidential elections to seek its support, though was not as direct in calling for the MB's recognition as a legal political force, in direct contrast to his political rival Ayman Nour.

Support for the MB's drive towards legitimacy appeared to have grown in intellectual circles within Egypt. Amr Choubaky, a leading analyst of the MB, has stated:

> It is possible to integrate them. But this requires first a serious democratic process which integrates political activists generally, and then, on the Brothers' side, they have to decide to choose between *al-da'wa* [the religious movement] and *al haraka al-siyasiya* [the political movement]. (International Crisis Group, interview, 4 October 2005, p. 26)

Choubaky was impressed by the new generation of MB members, who developed a discourse away from the movement's traditional religiosity, but believed there needed to be further changes to allow the new generation a greater role in decision-making and to form a programme for a civil political party (Choubaky, interview, 2004). The same view was presented by Mohammed El Said Said, deputy director of the Al-Ahram Center for Political and Strategic Studies, who insisted it is important for the MB to become a civil party rather than a religious movement, in order to minimise the risk of sectarian violence in Egypt (El Said, interview, 2004). The likelihood of the MB transforming itself comprehensively into a political movement seemed minimal, however, given the old guard's views and, at the grassroots level, the central role of its religious missionary work – the core of its broader social activism. The formation of a separate political organisation was a more likely option, as this would allow the MB to continue with its religious work while also presenting itself as a political movement detached from the spiritual. This was a crucial debate within the MB between the old guard and the new generation, one central to its future direction.

Overall, it is evident that the MB was able to win over opposition actors in its quest for legitimacy, making it difficult for Gamal Mubarak to sustain his position on the MB, which showed its political weight through its influence and impact on the succession process (see Chapter 7). This problem for Gamal was acknowledged through his attempts to neutralise the MB's new-generation leadership, but he was unwilling to go the extra yard and contemplate a legal platform for the movement in Egypt.

Conclusion

This chapter has explored the debates and pressures concerning economic and political reform in contemporary Egypt. It has examined the electoral promises made by Hosni Mubarak, and analysed the progress made in relation to those promises. As Egypt retreated into further authoritarianism, the demand for economic and political reform grew. Mubarak's economic pledges – to raise living standards and to create employment – came under criticism, given the prospect of further economic liberalisation and privatisation. With respect to the economic and political implications of the political succession, it seemed likely that the economic programme adopted in 1991 would continue, with liberalisation and privatisation continuing, albeit cautiously. Politically, little change was expected: Gamal was installed in the power hierarchy from 2000, and, since then, no real political change took place. In particular, there was not a drastic break with the governments past political position towards the MB, and no major change in their mutual relations. It seemed clear that Egypt under Gamal would not see a radical change from the economic and political agenda pursued under his father.

9

CONCLUSION

This book has explored the process of economic and political change in Egypt, with particular reference to the period 1991–2006, and through an examination of the MB and of the politics of the Egyptian succession. The case of Egypt was located in the context of broader economic and political changes in the Middle East, and four important questions were addressed. First, to what extent has there been a process of economic and political reform in Egypt? Second, to what extent has the process of economic and political change allowed for the emergence of a functioning civil society? Third, to what extent has this allowed political actors such as the MB to challenge state power? And finally, to what extent might the role of the MB be symptomatic of a challenge to the legitimacy of the existing state dispensation?

Chapter 2 explored economic and political reform in the context of the wider Middle East. In addition, this chapter located the discussion in the context of regional and global developments, such as US foreign policy after 11 September 2001 ('9/11') and the subsequent 'War on Terror'. Chapter 2 demonstrated that the process of limited political liberalisation evident in the region in the 1990s was reflective of a desire on the part of power elites to survive in the context of internal socio-economic pressures. Thus, the process of limited political change was insufficient on its own to allow oppositional actors to challenge the power and hegemony of the state; they were outmanoeuvred by institutions accustomed to survival, and they lacked a strong social support base to launch a challenge to state power. On the other hand, the process of limited political change driven by states' survival tactics, and by the need for a certain level of perceived legitimacy, provided room for Islamist parties to enter and play a role in the political system. This, and their presence in civil society outside that system – via involvement in trade unions, professional syndicates, student unions and teaching clubs – allowed the Islamists a establish a strong position from which to challenge state power. They took advantage of poor socio-economic conditions to do so, and their strength was boosted by regional crises such as the Palestinian-Israeli conflict, the 1991 Gulf War and the Algerian military coup of the early 1990s. Post-9/11, US foreign policy and the 'War on Terror', resulting in conflict in Afghanistan and Iraq, gave Islamists further opportunities to use these regional crises to strengthen their positions and launch direct challenges to state power. In addition, Israel's bombardment of Lebanon in 2006 and its incursions into the Gaza strip, together with US pressures on Iran and Syria, have only added to the strength of Islamist parties, which continue to act as counterweights to state power in the region. The discussion in Chapter 2 aimed to provide an understanding of economic and political change at the state and regional level, and a platform to examine the case of Egypt in Chapters 3–8.

Chapter 3 explored the process of economic and political reform in Egypt since 1991, in particular its impact on the power and structure of the state. The process of economic reform coincided with a process of political de-liberalisation. Most political actors, in particular the opposition, were paralysed by state intrusion into political life. However, despite this, the MB was able to escape political extinction and to grow and challenge the government; the reasons for this include the movement's structure, social base, changing shape and character, and its broad involvement in

Egyptian society. Given the important role the MB came to play in the 1990s, in challenging the Egyptian government and its power, Chapters 4–6 focused on how the movement was able to become a key political actor in Egypt and to challenge state hegemony. These chapters examined the details of the MB's transformation from a religious movement into a central political actor in Egyptian politics; they explored how the movement emerged as a strong political force and how internal organisational reforms contributed to its increasing strength and power in the country's political life. The internal political and organisational transformations inside the MB were situated alongside shifts in the spiritual and ideological discourse that it promoted. This is important, as by understanding these shifts, the process of change in the MB's shape and character and how it has come to relate to the Egyptian state can be more readily understood. These developments were looked at in particular through the role of the MB in two key Egyptian institutions: the parliament and the professional syndicates.

In particular, the MB used the professional syndicates to challenge the power and hegemony of the Egyptian state. At a time of socio-economic crisis in the 1990s, this was a dangerous situation for the government since these syndicates, historically, have played an important role in challenging state power and holding it to account. In response, the state intervened to paralyse the syndicates, and importantly to weaken thereby the growing influence and power of the MB. This was initially to be achieved by introducing Law 100, in 1993. After the failure of this to hinder the progress of the MB, it was amended by the government in 1995, but this also failed. The Egyptian state's next move was to take control of many syndicate boards, such as those of the medical and engineers' syndicates. However, despite this attempt to weaken it, the MB was able to continue with its challenge to the state, due to its large social support-base and its wide presence in civil society. The ability of the MB to contest state power and to contribute to the process of political reform was also facilitated by its willingness to cross ideological barriers. It tried to construct alliances (both political and civilian) and to add diversity to its social base. This can be seen clearly post-2000, as the MB tried to have an impact on the process of political succession in Egypt.

This discussion of the MB was followed in Chapters 7 and 8 by an analysis of the politics of succession. This became an important issue after 2000, dominated by the increasing role and power of Gamal Mubarak. The rise of Gamal and his associates to the upper echelons of Egyptian politics raised many questions concerning the future of economic and political change in the country, and it was therefore important to present the discourse surrounding the political succession, taking into consideration the actors involved and the forces driving the process. In addition, it was also important to examine key political actors, such as the MB, to determine the extent of their influence on the political succession process. Since 2000 the MB was vocal in its criticism of this process, and its impact was strengthened through its willingness to join forces with new social-protest movements such as *Kefayah* and the communist party. These alliances between the MB and other social forces heightened the concerns of the Egyptian state, and these escalated when the movement began to take to the streets to galvanise public support in opposition to the succession process. In reaction to these developments the government resorted to coercion; however, this failed to weaken the MB, once again because of its presence both inside and outside the political system. As a result, the government shifted its policy, pursuing a strategy of attempting to neutralise the MB and thus to halt its challenge to the succession process. The struggle between the government and the MB crystallised in the context of the succession process.

The politics of succession allows an understanding of the forces involved in the power struggle that unfolded in Egypt, and provides a platform from which to examine the future process of economic and political change in the country, in particular the level of continuity or discontinuity. Relating questions of reform

to the weight of the MB and the politics of succession is important for a number of reasons. First, it allows an understanding of
the process of economic and political change in the country and
its impact on the MB, which led it to challenge state power in
the 1990s. Post-2000 the movement continued to confront the
government, through its ability to influence the political succession process. Second, focusing on the changing character of the
MB sheds light on the transition of Islamism in Egypt and the
wider Middle East. The internal changes and transformations of
the MB, as a leading Islamic movement, have had an impact on
Islamist parties in the region, such as the IAF in Jordan, the JDP
in Morocco, and even Hamas in the Palestinian Territories. Third,
the focus on the politics of succession provides insight into the level
of continuity and discontinuity in future processes of economic
and political reform.

Economic reform in Egypt had continued to be market-domi-
nated, with the rise of Gamal Mubarak speeding up the process
of economic liberalisation, in particular the building of links to
wider markets. As a result, there was a great deal of emphasis in
Egypt on developing the stock and capital markets, in order to
improve their competence and to attract regional and international investors. While the process of economic reform remained
market-centric, Gamal extended this to include regional and
global markets. Meanwhile, the process of political reform indicated both continuity and discontinuity, in terms of shifts between
political liberalisation and de-liberalisation. This formed the basis
of the Egyptian government's political strategy, in order both to
balance the political weight of the MB and to manage the process
of political succession.

The overall argument in this book has been that Egypt in the
1990s underwent a process of economic and political change. This
period of change coincided with a socio-economic crisis, which
was worsened by economic reforms carried out by the government
under the influence of the IMF and WB. These reforms led to the

development of internal socio-economic pressures which threatened the power and legitimacy of the government, which, in order to survive, sustained a process of political de-liberalisation. This was aimed at weakening the growing political power and influence of the MB – the state was mindful of the movement's growing strength in civil society. The existence of the MB both inside and outside the political system allowed it to pressure the government, which, concerned at the challenge to its power and legitimacy, resorted to coercive action.

This concern about the political weight of the MB, in combination with the growing socio-economic demands of the Egyptian people, posed survival dilemmas to the government. This can be clearly seen in the context of the politics of succession, as the government sought to manage the process carefully in order to deal both with the MB and with rising socio-economic demands. Despite this careful management and planning by the government, there was widespread opposition to the political succession process in Egypt, as seen in the run-up to the 2005 elections and in the ensuing period. This opposition resulted in the government further tightening its control over society, to ensure the process continued unimpeded. Given this political reality, apparent since the 2005 elections, the process of economic and political change in Egypt were dictated by three main factors. These were internal socio-economic demands, the political weight of the MB, and the politics of succession. The last of these is a key factor behind recent economic and political developments in the country, and was vital not only in determining relations between the Egyptian state and the MB, but also, by its very nature, in the nature of political reform.

REFERENCES

Primary sources
Interviews

Choubaky, A, *Expert in Islamism and Islamic Movements*, Centre for Political and Strategic Studies, Al Ahram, Cairo, May 1st, 2004.

El Fattah, N, *Civil Society Expert*, Centre for Political and Strategic Studies, Al Ahram, Cairo, July 5th, 2004.

El Said, M, *Leading Egyptian Intellectual*, Centre for Political and Strategic Studies, Al Ahram, Cairo, April 20th, 2004.

Hamzawy, A, *Expert on Islamic Movements*, Cairo University, Cairo, June 1st, 2004 (Now Senior Research Fellow at the Carnegie Endowment Centre for International Peace and Democracy, Washington, US).

Kish, H, *Senior Member of the Tagammu Party and Researcher*, Centre for Criminological and Sociological Research, Cairo, May 5th, 2004.

Madi, Abul Ella, *Former Senior Member of the Muslim Brotherhood and now the leader of Hizb al Wasat* (The Centre Party), Cairo, May 20th, 2004.

Nafa, H, *Professor of Political Science*, Cairo University, Cairo, May 17th, 2004.

Qandil, A, *Civil Society and Human Rights Activist*, Cairo, July 6th, 2004.

Rishwan, D, *Expert on Islamism and Islamic Movements*, Centre for Political and Strategic Studies, Al Ahram, Cairo, June 4th, 2004.

Secondary sources
Books

Abdel Haleem, M (2004), *The Qur'an / A New Translation*, Oxford: Oxford University Press.

Abdel-Malek, K (2000), *America in Arab Mirror Images of America in Arabic Travel Literature, an Anthology (1895–1995)* New York: St. Martin's Press.

Abdel Rahman, M (2004), *Civil Society Exposed, the Politics of NGOs in Egypt*, Cairo: American University in Cairo Press.

Al-Awadi, H (2004), *In Pursuit of Legitimacy: the Muslim Brothers and Mubarak, 1982–2000,* London: I.B.Tauris.

Ayubi, N (1991), *Political Islam; Religion and Politics in the Arab world,* London: Routledge.

Ayubi, N (1991), *The State and Public Policies in Egypt since Sadat,* Ithaca Press.

Ayubi, N (1995), *Over Stating the Arab state: Politics and Society in the Middle East,* London: I.B.Tauris.

Baker, R (1990), *Sadat and After: Struggles for Egypt's Political Soul,* Cambridge: Harvard University Press.

Baker, R (2003), *Islam without Fear; Egypt and the New Islamists,* Cambridge: Harvard University Press.

Bari, Z (1995), *Re-Emergence of the Muslim Brothers in Egypt,* New Delhi: Lancers Books.

Bayyumi, Z (1979), *Al Ikhwan al Muslimeen,* (the Muslim Brothers), Cairo: Maktabat Wahba.

Beattie, K (2000), *Egypt during the Sadat years,* New York and Hampshire: Palgrave.

Bensahel, N and Byman, D (2004), *The Future Security Environment in the Middle East; Conflict, Stability and Political Change* (Eds), Washington: RAND Project.

Bianchi, R (1989), *Unruly Corporatism: Associational Life in 20th Century Egypt,* New York: Oxford University Press.

Bird, G (1995), *IMF lending to Developing Countries: Issues and Evidence,* London: Routledge.

Bromley, S (1994), *Rethinking Middle East Politics: State Formation and Development,* Blackwell Publishers.

Bush, R (1999), *Economic Crisis and the Policies of Reform in Egypt,* Boulder: West View Press.

Bush, R (2002), *Counter Revolution in Egypt's Countryside; Land and Farmers in the Era of Economic Reform,* New York: Zed Books.

Clark, J (2004), *Islam, Charity, and Activism,* Bloomington: Indian University Press.

Dessouki, H (1982), *Islamic Resurgence in the Arab World,* New York: Praeger Publishers.

Dresch, P (2000), *A History of Modern Yemen,* Cambridge University Press.

Easterly, W (2001), *The Elusive Quest for Growth; Economists Adventures and Misadventures in the Tropics,* MIT Press.

Crystal, J (1990), *Oil and Politics in the Gulf: Rulers and Merchants in Kuwait and Qatar,* Cambridge University Press.

Esposito, J (2002), *Unholy War: Terror in the Name of Islam,* Oxford University Press.

Fahmy, N (2002), *The Politics of Egypt: State-Society Relationship,* Richmond: Curzon.

Friedman, M (1962), *Capitalism and Freedom,* University of Chicago Press.

Fuller, G (2003), *The Future of Political Islam,* New York: Palgrave Macmillan.

Erian, M, Eken, S and Fennell, S and Chanffour, J (1996), *Growth and Stability in the Middle East and North Africa,* Washington: IMF.

Gellner, E (1994), *Conditions of Liberty: Civil Society and its Enemies,* New York: Penguin.

Gilsenan, M (1973), *Saint and Sufi in Modern Egypt: an Essay in the Sociology of Religion,* Oxford: Oxford University Press.

Goldberg, E (1986), *Tinker, Tailor, and Textile Worker: Class and Politics in Egypt, 1930–1952,* Los Angeles: University of California Press.

Guazzone, L (1995), *The Islamist Dilemma: the Political Role of Islamist Movements in the Contemporary Arab world,* Berkshire: Ithaca Press.

Handoussa, H and Potter, G (1991), *Employment and Structural Adjustment: Egypt in the 1990s,* Cairo: American University in Cairo Press.

Harik, I (1997), *Economic Policy Reform in Egypt,* Gainesville: University of Florida Press.

Harik, I and Sullivan, D (1992), *Privatisation and Liberalisation in the Middle East,* Bloomington and Indianapolis: Indiana University Press.

Harris, C (1964), *Nationalism and Revolution in Egypt: The Role of the Muslim Brotherhood,* The Hague: Mouton.

Hasan, A.H (2000), *Al Su'ud al-Siyasi al-Islami dakhil al-Niqabat al-Mihaniyya,* (The Islamic Political Ascent Inside Professional Syndicates), Cairo: al Dar al Saqafia Li al Kasher.

Hayek, F (1960), *The Constitution of Liberty,* Chicago: University of Chicago Press.

Hinnebusch, R (1985), *Egyptian Politics under Sadat: the Post-Populist Development of an Authoritarian Modernizing State,* Cambridge University Press.

Hinnebusch, R (2001), *Syria: Revolution from Above,* London, Routledge.

Hopwood, D (1993), *Egypt: Politics and Society, 1949–1990,* Routledge.

Hudaybi, H (1977), *Du'a La Quda,* (Preachers not Judges), Cairo: Tarbiya Publishing.

Husani Musa, I (1956), *The Moslem Brethren: the Greatest of Modern Islamic Movements,* Beirut Publishers.

Hussain, A (1988), *Political Terrorism and the State in the Middle East,* London and New York: Mansell Publishing Limited.

Jameelah, M (1980), *Shaikh Hassan al Banna wa al-Ikhwan al-Muslimeen,* (Hassan Al Banna and the Muslim Brotherhood), Mohammed Yusuf Khan and Sons.

Jankowski, J (2001), *Nasser's Egypt: Arab Nationalism and the United Arab Republic,* Lynne Reiner.

Kepel, G (2002), *Jihad: The Trial of Political Islam,* Belknap Press.

Khatab, S (2006), *The Power of Sovereignty: The Political and Ideological Philosophy of Sayyid Qutb,* New York: Routledge.

Kienle, E (2001), *A Grand Delusion: Democracy and Economic Reform in Egypt*, London: I.B.Tauris.

Kienle, E (2004), *Politics from Above, Politics from Below: The Middle East in the Age of Economic Reform*, Saqi Books.

Killick, T (1995), *IMF Programmes in Developing Countries: Design and Impact*, London: Routledge.

Kramer, M (1996), *Arab Awakening and Islamic Revival; the Politics of Ideas in the Middle East*, New Brunswick: Transaction Publishers.

Leverett, F (2005), *Inheriting Syria: Bashar's Trial by Fire*, Brookings Institute Press.

Lia, B (1998), *The Society of the Muslim Brothers in Egypt: The Rise of an Islamic Mass Movement, 1928–1942*, Ithaca Press.

Maye, K (2004), *Egyptian Politics: The Dynamics of Authoritarian Rule*, Lynne Reiner.

McDermott, A (1989), *Egypt from Nasser to Mubarak: a Flawed Revolution*, London: Croom Helm.

Mitchell, R (1969), *The Society of Muslim Brothers*, Oxford University Press.

Mousalli, A (1992), *Radical Islamic Fundamentalism: The Ideological and Political Discourse of Sayyid Qutb*, Beirut: American University of Beirut Press.

Niblock, T and Murphy, E (1993), *Economic and Political Liberalisation in the Middle East*, London British Academy Press.

Norton, A (1995–96), *Civil Society in the Middle East*, Leiden: Brill.

O'Brien, M (2002), *Six Days of War: June 1967 and the Making of the Modern Middle East*, Oxford University Press.

Posusney, M (2005), *Authoritarianism in the Middle East: Regimes and Resistance*, Lynne Rienner.

Qandil, A (1995), *The Process of Democratisation in Egypt (1981–1993)*, Cairo: Ibn Khaldun Center for Development Studies.

Qutb, S (1991), *Milestones*, American Trust Publications.

Qutb, S (2000), *The America I Have Seen*, New York.

Qutb, S (2002), *In the Shade of the Qur'an*, (Translated and Edited by Adil Salahi) Vol 5, United Kingdom: The Islamic Foundation.

Rahnema, A (1994), *Pioneers of Islamic Revival*, London: Zed books.

Richards, A (2001), *The Political Economy of Economic Reform in the Middle East: The Challenge of Governance*, Washington: RAND Project.

Richards, A and Waterbury, J (1996), *A Political Economy of the Middle East*, (2nd Ed), Boulder: West View Press.

Richards, A and Waterbury, J (1990), *A Political Economy of the Middle East; State, Class and Economic Development*, Boulder: West View Press.

Rivlin, P (1985), *The Dynamics of Economic Policy Making in Egypt*, New York: Praeger.

Rubin, B (1990), *Islamic Fundamentalism and Egyptian Politics*, New York: St Martin's Press.

Rumaihi, T (1997), *Al-Wasat wa al-Ikhwan* (al-Wasat Party and the Muslim Brotherhood), Cairo: Markaz Yafa.

Salame, G (1994), *Democracy without Democrats? The Renewal of Politics in the Muslim World*, London: I.B.Tauris.

Seale, P (1990), *Asad of Syria: The Struggle for the Middle East,* University of California Press.

Shafiq, N (1998), *Prospects for Middle Eastern and North African Economies: from Boom to Bust and Back?* London: Macmillan.

Shephard, W (1996), *Sayyid Qutb and Islamic Activism: A Translation and Critical Analysis of Social Justice in Islam,* New York: E.J.Brill.

Simon, S and Benjamin, D (2002), *The Age of Sacred Terror: Radical Islam's War Against America,* New York: Random House.

Stephens, R (1973), *Nasser: A Political Biography,* Harmondsworth: Penguin Books.

Thompson, E. P. (1972), *The Making of the English Working Class,* Harmondsworth: Penguin.

Tripp, C and Owen, R (1991), *Egypt under Mubarak,* London: Routledge.

Waterbury, J (1983), *The Egypt of Nasser and Sadat: The Political Economy of Two Regimes,* Princeton University Press.

Wickham, C (2002), *Mobilising Islam: Religion, Activism and Political Change in Egypt,* New York: Columbia University Press.

Woodward, P (1992), *Nasser,* London; New York: Longman.

Yakran, F (1998), *Manhajiyat al-Imam Hassan al-Banna wa madaris al-Ikhwan al-Muslimeen* (The Methodology of the martyred Imam Hassan al Banna and the schools of the Muslim Brotherhood), Beirut: Al Risala Publishers.

Zaki, M (1995), *Civil Society and Democratisation in Egypt, 1981–1994,* Cairo: Konrad-Adenauer Stiftung/ the Ibn Khaldun Centre.

Zisser, E (2000), *Asad's Legacy: Syria in Transition,* New York University Press.

Chapters in Books

Abdel Khalek, G (1992), 'Egypt's ERSAP: The Orthodox Recipe and The Alternative', in (Eds) Abdel Khalek, G and El-Dien, H.K, *Economic Reform and its Distributional Impacts,* Cairo: Dar El-Mostaqbal El-Arabi.

Ayubi, N (1988), 'Domestic Politics', in (Eds) Harris, L, *Egypt: Internal Challenges and Regional Stability,* London, Routledge and Kegan Paul.

Chiriboga, M (2002), 'Latin American NGO's and the IFI's: the Quest for a South Determined Agenda', in (Eds) Scholte, J.A and Schabel, A, *Civil Society and Global Finance,* London: Routledge.

Clark, J (2000), 'The Economic and Political Impact of Economic Restructuring on NGO-State Relations in Egypt', in (Eds) Kleinberg, R.B and Clark, J, *Economic Liberalisation, Democratisation and Civil Society in the Developing World,* London: Macmillan Press LTD and New York: ST. Martin's Press. pp.157–179.

El-Laithy, H (1997), 'Structural Adjustment and Poverty', in (Eds) El-Mahdied, A, *Aspects of Structural Adjustment in Africa and Egypt*, Cairo: Cairo University, Center for Political Research and Studies. pp.131–199.

El-Mahdi, A (1997), 'The Economic Reform Program in Egypt after Four Years of Implementation', in (Eds) El-Mahdied, A, *Aspects of Structural Adjustment in Africa and Egypt*, Cairo: Center for Political Research and Studies, Cairo University, pp.15–56.

Galal, A and Tohamy, S (1998,), 'Toward an Egypt-U.S. Free Trade Agreement, an Egyptian Perspective', in (Eds) Galal, A and Lawrence, R, *Building Bridges: an Egypt-U.S. Free Trade Agreement*, Washington: Brookings Institution Press. pp.13–36

Gilsenan, M (1985), 'Trajectories of Contemporary Sufism', in (Eds) Gellner, E, *Islamic Dilemmas: Reformers, Nationalists and Industrialization*, Amsterdam: Mouton, pp.187–198.

Haddad, Y (1983), 'Sayyid Qutb: Ideologue of Islamic Revival', in (Eds) Esposito, J, *Voices of Resurgent Islam*, New York, Oxford University Press.

Ibrahim, S (1995), 'Civil Society and Prospects for Democratisation in the Middle East', in (Eds) Norton, A, *Civil Society in the Middle East*, Leiden: Brill.

Langhor, V (2005), 'Too Much Civil Society, Too little Politics? Egypt and other Liberalizing Arab Regimes', in (Eds) Posusney, M and Penner Angrist, M, *Authoritarianism in the Middle East*, Lynne Reinner.

Mardin, S (1995), 'Civil society and Islam', in (Eds) Hall, J, *Civil Society: History, Theory, Comparison*, Cambridge: Polity Press.

Mohieldin, M and Nasr, S (1996), 'On Privatization in Egypt: With Reference to the Experience of the Czech Republic and Mexico', in (Eds) Wadouda, B and Wahby, A, *Privatization in Egypt: the Debate in the People's Assembly*, Cairo: Center for Political Research and Studies, Cairo University, pp. 16–71.

Mustafa, H (1995), 'The Islamist Movement under Mubarak', in (Eds) Guazzone, L, *The Islamist Dilemma; the Political Role of Islamist Movements in the Contemporary Arab World*, Berkshire: Ithaca Press.

Qandil, A (1996), 'Occupational Groups and Political Participation', in (Eds), El Sayid, M, *The Reality of Political Pluralism in Egypt*, Cairo: Madbouli.

Shukrallah, H (1989), 'Political Crisis and Political Conflict in Post 1967 Egypt', in (Eds) Owen, R and Tripp, C, *Egypt under Mubarak*, London: Routledge, p.94.

Wickham, C (1996), 'Islamic Mobilisation and Political Change: The Islamist Trend in Egypt's Professional Associations', in (Eds) Beinin, J and Stork, J, *Political Islam: Essays from the Middle East Report*, University of California Press, pp.120–136.

Williamson, J (1990), 'What Washington Means by Policy Reform', in (Eds) Williamson, J, *Latin American Adjustment: How Much Has Happened?* Washington: Institute for International Economics.

Williamson, J (1996), 'Are the Latin American Reforms Sustainable?', in (Eds) Sautter, H and Schinke, R, *Stabilization and Reforms in Latin America: Where Do We Stand?* Frankfurt: Vervuert Verlag.

Williamson, J (1997), 'The Washington Consensus Revisited', in (Eds) Emmerij, L, *Economic and Social Development into the XXI Century*, Washington: Inter-American Development Bank.

Zubaida, S (2001), 'Civil Society, Community, and Democracy in the Middle East', in (Eds) Kaviraj, S and Khilnani, S, *Civil Society: History and Possibilities*, Cambridge University Press, pp.232–49.

Journal Articles

Abd al Monein, S and Wenner, M (1982), 'Modern Islamic Reform Movements; The Muslim Brotherhood in contemporary Egypt', *Middle East Journal*, Summer, Vol 36, pp.353.

Abdel Khalek, G (1993), 'Structural Reform or Dutch Disease?', *L'Egypte Contemporaine*, July-October No. 433–434, pp.5–53.

Abdel Kotob, S (1995), 'The Accommodationists Speak; Goal and Strategies of the Muslim Brotherhood in Egypt', *International Journal of Middle East Studies*, Vol, 27, pp.321–339.

Abdel Rahman, M (2002), 'Politics of "Un-Civil" Society in Egypt', *Review of African Political Economy*, March. Vol 29, No 91.

Aboul Enein, Y (2003), 'Al Ikhwan al Muslimeen: The Muslim Brotherhood', *Military Review*, July-August, pp.26–31

Aboul, Enien, Y (2004), 'The Egyptian-Yemen War: Egyptian perspectives on Guerrilla Warfare', *Infantry Magazine*, January–February.

Ahmad, I (1996), 'Intellectual Origins of Islamic Resurgence in the Modern Arab World', *Arab Studies Quarterly*, Summer.

Albrecht, H and Schlumberger, O (2004), 'Waiting for Godot: Regime Change without Democratisation in the Middle East', *International Political Science Review*, Vol 25, No 4, pp.371–392.

Albright, M (2003), 'Bridges, Bombs or Blusters?', *Foreign Affairs*, September/October, Issue 83. pp.22–31.

Altman, I (2006), 'Current Trends in the Ideology of the Muslim Brotherhood', *Journal Current Trends in Islamist Ideology*, January, Vol 3. pp.30–38.

Amin, J (1998), 'Major Determinants of Economic Development in Egypt: 1977–1997', *Cairo Papers in Social Science*, Vol 21.

Aoude, I (1994), 'From National Bourgeois Development to Infitah: Egypt 1952–1992', *Arab Studies Quarterly (ASQ)*, Winter, Vol 16, No.1.

Barraclough, S (1998), 'Al Azhar between the Government and the Islamists', *Middle East Journal*, Spring, Vol 52 No 2, pp.236–249.

Bayat, A (1998), 'Revolution without Movement, Movement without Revolution: Comparing Islamic Activism in Iran and Egypt', *Comparative Studies in Society and History*, January, Vol 40, No 1, pp.136–139.

Beinin, J (2005), 'Political Islam and the New Global Economy: The Political Economy of an Egyptian Social Movement', *The New Centennial Review*, 5.1, pp.111–139.

Berman, S (2003), 'Islamism, Revolution and Civil Society', *Perspectives on Politics*, 1.2, pp.257–72.

Brownlee, J (2002), 'The Decline of Pluralism in Mubarak's Egypt', *Journal of Democracy*, October, No 13.4, pp.6–14.

Brumberg, D (2002), 'The Trap of Liberalized Autocracy', *Journal of Democracy*, No 13.4, pp.56–68.

Brumberg, D (2002), 'Islamists and the Politics of Consensus', *Journal of Democracy*, Vol. 13, No. 3, pp.109–115.

Burke, E (1987), 'Understanding Arab Protest Movements', *Arab Studies Quarterly*, Fall, Vol 8, pp.333–345.

Campagna, J (1996), 'From Accommodation to Confrontation: the Muslim Brotherhood in the Mubarak Years', *Journal of Public Affairs*, Vol 50, No 27.

Cavatorta, F (2006), 'Civil Society, Islamism and Democratisation: the Case of Morocco', *Journal of Modern African Studies*, Vol 44, pp.203–222.

Cook, S (2005), 'The Right Way to Promote Arab Reform', *Foreign Affairs*, March/April, Vol 84, No 2, pp.91–102.

Dalacoura, K (2005), 'US Democracy Promotion in the Arab Middle East, since 11th September 2001: a Critique', *International Affairs*, Vol 81, No 5, October, p.963.

Dhumale, R (2000), 'Public Investment in the Middle East and North Africa; Towards Fiscal Efficiency', *Development Policy Review*, Vol 18, pp.307–324.

Ehteshami, A (2003), 'A Reform from Above; the Politics of Participation in the Oil Monarchies', *International Affairs*, Vol 79, No 1, pp.53–75.

Esposito, J (1993/1994), 'Political Islam and American Foreign Policy', *Brown Journal of World Affairs*, Vol 1, No 1, pp.63–82.

Fahmy, N (1998), 'The Performance of the Muslim Brotherhood in the Egyptian Syndicates: An alternative Formula for Reform?', *Middle East Journal*, Vol 52, No 4, autumn, pp.551–562.

Freedman, M (2004), 'Islamism and Nationalism: The Rise of Islamic Fundamentalism in the 20th Century', *Undergraduate Quarterly*, November.

Gambill, G (2000), 'The Assad family and the Succession in Syria', *Middle East Intelligence Bulletin*, July, Vol 2, No 6.

Gambill, G (2001), 'The Political Obstacles to Economic Reform in Syria', *Middle East Intelligence Bulletin*, July, Vol 3, No 7.

Gambill, G (2004), 'The Myth of Syria's Old Guard', *Middle East Intelligence Bulletin*, February-March, Vol 6, No. 2/3.

Gambill, G (2003), 'Explaining the Arab Democracy Deficit', *Middle East Intelligence Bulletin*, February-March, Vol 5, No 2.

Gardner, E (2003), 'Wanted: More Jobs', *Finance and Development Quarterly Magazine of the IMF*, March, Vol 40, No 1, pp.8–21.

Gause, G (2005), 'Can Democracy Stop Terrorism?', *Foreign Affairs*, September/ October, Vol 84, No. 5, pp.62–76.

Gilsenan, M (1967), 'Some Factors in the Decline of Sufi Orders in Modern Egypt', *The Muslim World*, No 57, pp.11–18.

Goodson, L and Radwan, S (1997), 'Democratisation in Egypt in the 1990s Stagnant, or Merely Stunted?', *Arab Studies Quarterly*, Winter, np.

Harb, I (2003), 'The Egyptian Military in Politics: Disengagement or Accommodation?', *Middle East Journal*, Vol 57, No. 2, pp.297–316.

Henzel, C (2005), 'The Origins of Al Qaeda's Ideology: Implications for US Strategy Parameters', *US Army War College Quarterly*, Spring.

Herb, M (2002), 'Democratisation in the Arab world? Emirs and Parliaments in the Gulf', *Journal of Democracy*, October, Vol 13, No 4, pp.41–47.

Herb, M (2005), 'No Representation without Taxation? Rents, Development and Democracy', *Comparative Politics*, Vol 37, No 3.

Ibrahim, S (1988), 'Egypt's Islamic activism in the 1980s', *Third World Quarterly*, April, Vol 10, No 2, pp.632–657.

Kechichian, J (2004), 'Democratisation in Gulf Monarchies: A New Challenge to the GCC', *Middle East Policy*, Winter, Vol 11, No 4, pp.37–57.

Khan, M (1998), 'US Foreign Policy and Political Islam; Interests, Ideas and Ideology', *Security Dialogue*, Vol 29, No 4, December, pp.449–462.

Kienle, E (1998), 'More than a Response to Islamism: The Political Deliberalisation of Egypt in the 1990s', *Middle East Journal*, Spring, Vol 52, No 2, pp.219–235.

Langhor, V (2001), 'Of Islamist and Ballot Boxes, Rethinking the Relationship Between Islamists and Electoral Politics', *International Journal of Middle East Studies*, November, Vol 33, No 4 pp.591–610.

Ledeen, M (2002), 'If you want to win the War, win the Debate', *Wall Street Journal*, September 4th.

Lofgren, H (1993), 'Economic Policy in Egypt: A breakdown in Reform Assistance', *International Journal of Middle East Studies*, Vol 25, pp.407–421.

Mattoon, S (1992), 'Islam by Profession', *The Middle East*, Vol 3, No. 218, December 16th.

McGregor, A (2003), 'Jihad and the Rifle Alone, Abdullah Azzam and the Islamic Revolution', *Journal of Conflict Studies*, Fall, Vol 23, No. 2. p.103.

Moustafa, T (2000), 'Conflict and Cooperation between the State and Religious Institutions in Contemporary Egypt', *International Journal Middle Eastern Studies*, Vol 32, pp.3–22.

Munson, Z (2001), 'Islamic Mobilisation: Social Movement Theory and the Egyptian Muslim Brotherhood', *The Sociological Quarterly*, Vol 42, No 4, pp.487–510.

Nassar, S.Z. and Fawzy, H. R, (1993), 'Impacts of the Economic Reform Policies on Food Production in Egypt', *L'Egypte Contemporaine*, No 432, April, pp.5–43.

Neep, D (2004), 'Dilemmas of Democratisation in the Middle East: The Forward Strategy of Freedom', *Middle East Policy*, Fall, Vol 11, No 3, pp.73–84.

Nonneman, G (2001), 'State of the Art – Rentiers and Autocrats, Monarchs, and Democrats, State and Society: the Middle East between Globalizing, Human "Agency" and Europe', *International Affairs*, Vol 77, No 1, pp.141–162.

Nufrio, P (2004), 'Examining the September 11th Terrorist Attacks, Can Democracy and Economic Development purge the Clash of Civilisation', *Public Administration and Management: An Interactive Journal*, Vol 9, No 1, pp.70–86.

Olav Utvik, B (2005), 'Hizb al-Wasat and the Potential for Change in Egyptian Islamism Critique', *Critical Middle Eastern Studies*, Vol. 14, No. 3, Fall, pp.293–306.

Posusney, M (2004), 'Enduring authoritarianism', *Comparative Politics 36*, 2, pp.127–38.

Pratt, N (2004), 'Bringing Politics Back In: Examining the Link between Globalization and Democratisation', *Review of International Political Economy*, Vol 11, No 2, pp.331–336.

Pratt, N (2004), 'Understanding Political Transformation in Egypt: Advocacy NGOs, Civil Society and the State', *Journal of Mediterranean Studies*, Vol 14(1/2), pp.237–262.

Richards, A (1991), 'The Political Economy of Dilatory Reform: Egypt in the 1980s', *World Development*, December, Vol 19, No 12, pp.1721–1730.

Rumaihi, M (1996), 'The Gulf Monarchies: Testing Time', *The Middle East Quarterly*, December, Vol 3, No 4, pp.45–51.

Ryan, C (1998), 'Peace, Bread and Riots: Jordan and the International Monetary Fund', *Middle East Policy*, October, Vol 6, No 2, pp.54–66.

Ryan, C (2001), 'Political Strategies and Regime Survival in Egypt', *Journal of Third World Studies*, Fall, pp.25–46.

Sadiki, L (1997), 'Towards Arab Liberal Governance: from the Democracy of the Bread to the Democracy of the Vote', *Third World Quarterly*, Vol 18, No 1, pp.127–148.

Sadiki, L (2000), 'Popular Uprisings and Arab Democratisation', *International Journal of Middle East Studies*, Vol 32, pp.71–95.

Seddon, D (1990), 'The Politics of Adjustment: Egypt and the IMF, 1987–1990', *Review of African Political Economy*, Spring, Vol 17, No, 47, pp.84–94.

Shehata, S (2002), 'Political Succession in Egypt', *Middle East Policy*, September, Vol 1V, No 3, pp.105–123.

Sid-Ahmed, M (1987–1988), 'Egypt: The Islamic Issue', *Foreign Policy*, Winter, No. 69, pp.22–39.

Sobelman, D (2001), 'Gamal Mubarak, President of Egypt?', *The Middle East Quarterly*, Spring, Vol V111, No 2, pp.31–40.

Sorenson, D (2003), 'The Dynamics of Political Dissent in Egypt', *The Fletcher Forum of World Affairs*, Summer/Fall, Vol 27, No 2.

Stacher, J (2002), 'Post Islamist Rumblings in Egypt: The Emergence of the Wasat Party', *The Middle East Journal*, Vol 56, pp.415–432.

Sullivan, D (1990), 'The Political Economy of Reform in Egypt', *International Journal of Middle East Studies*, Vol 22, pp.317–334.

Westley, J (1998), 'Change in Egyptian Economy, 1977–1997', *Cairo Papers in Social Science*, Vol 21.

Wickham, C (2004), 'The Problem with Coercive Democratisation: The Islamist Response to the U.S. Democracy Reform Initiative', *World Journal of Human Rights*, Vol. 1, Issue 1, October, np.

Windsor, J (2003), 'Promoting Democratisation can Combat Terrorism', *The Washington Quarterly*, Summer, 26:2, pp.43–58.

Wright, S (2006), 'Generational Change and Elite-driven Reforms in the Kingdom (Sir William Luce Fellowship Paper, No 7)', *Middle East and Islamic Studies*, University of Durham, np.

Zisser, E (2003), 'Does Bashar al Assad rule Syria?', *The Middle East Quarterly*, Vol 10, No.1, pp.15–23.

Zohny, A (1987), 'Towards an apolitical role for the Egyptian Military in the management of development', *Orient*, 4, p.548

Website Articles

Aboul Enein, Y (2006), 'The Concept of the Caliphate: A Key Islamic Militant Ideological Point, No 2', *Foreign Area Officer Association*, http://www.faoa.org

Arafa, M (2001), 'Niqabat al Muhamin al Misriyya, (The Egyptian Lawyers Syndicate)', *Islam Online*, 9 September, www.islamonline.net

Arafa, M (2001), 'Niqabat al-Muhandiseen: Bedayat Fard al-Hirasa 'ala al-Niqabat al-Misriyya, (The Engineers Syndicate: The beginning of judicial control over Egyptian Syndicates)', *Islam Online*, 24 July, www.islamonline.net

Bayat, A (2003), 'The Street and the Politics of Dissent in the Arab world', *Middle East Report Online*, Spring, No 226, http://www.merip.org/mer/mer226/226_bayat.html

Fergany, N (1998), 'The Growth of Poverty in Egypt', *Egypt: Al-Mishkat Centre for Research*, (Online), January, http://www.almishkat.org/engdoc98/rn12/rn12_00.htm

Ghobashy, M (2003), 'Egypt's Summer of Discontent', *Middle East Report Online*, September 18th, http://www.merip.org/mero/mero091803.html

Hirst, D (1999), 'Egypt Stands on Feet of Clay', (Online edition), *Le Monde Diplomatique*, October, http://mondediplo,com/1999/10/09egypt

Martin, J (2001), 'Egypt's Privatization Goes Nowhere', *The Middle East Online*, February, http://web1.infotrac.galegroup.com/itw/infomark/

NTDB, National Trade Data Bank, U.S Department of Commerce November 1997, Report dated 082197, *Egyptian Investment Climate Statement*, (Online) http://www.awo.net/business/invest/egy1.asp/

Philips, S (2005), 'Cracks in the Yemeni System', *Middle East Report Online*, July 28th, http://www.merip.org/mero/mero072805.html

Philips, S (2006), 'Foreboding about the Future in Yemen', *Middle East Report Online*, April 3rd, http://www.merip.org/mero/mero040306.html

Pingree, G (2005) 'Morocco's Rising Islamist Challenge', *Christian Science Monitor Online*, November 23, http://www.csmonitor.com/2005/1123/006s02-wome.html

Regan, T (2005), 'Does Democracy lead to an end of Terrorism?', *Christian Science Monitor Online*, October 20th, http://www.csmonitor.com/2005/1020/dailyUpdate.html

Ryan, C (2005), 'Reform Retreats Amid Jordan's Political Storms', *Middle East Report Online*, June 10th, http://www.merip.org/mero/mero061005.html

Schanzer, J (2002), 'Gamal Mubarak: Successor Story in Egypt?', *Policy Watch, the Washington Institute for Near East Policy*, No 669, October 17th, http://schanzer.pundicity.com/583/gamal-mubarak-successor-story-in-egypt

Schwedler, J (2002), 'Don't Blink Jordan's Democratic Opening and Closing', *Middle East Report Online*, July 3rd, http://www.merip.org/mero/mero070302.html

Schwedler, J (1998–1999), 'A Paradox of Democracy? Islamist Participation in Democratic Elections', *Middle East Report*, No. 209, Winter, pp.25–29, http://merip.org/mer/mer209/paradox-democracy

Speck, U (2006), 'Democracy Promotion in the Middle East and North Africa: Recent Experiences and Further Prospects', *AICGS Advisor*, May 12.

Zenati, H (2004), 'Mubarak, Republican Heir Apparent', *Middle East Online*, September 24th. http://www.middle-east-online.com/english/?id=11372

Reports and Conferences

Abdul Hafiz, A (2003), *Niqabat al-Muhamiyeen: Surat Misr fi al-Qarn al-'Ashreen* (The Lawyers Syndicate: Egypt's image in the 20th century). Cairo: Al Ahram Center for Political and Strategic Studies.

Abdalla, A (2003), *Egypt before and after September 11, 2001: Problems of Political Transformation in a Complicated International Setting*, Report – Deutsches Orient Institute.

Ahmed, A, Bouis, H, Gutner, T and Lofgren, H (2001), *The Egyptian Food Subsidy System Structure, Performance, and Options for Reform*, Research Report No. 119, International Food Policy Research Institute, Washington.

Al Sayid, M (2003), *Politics and Economic Growth in Egypt, 1950–2000*, Report, Centre for the Study of Developing Countries, Cairo University, July.

Arab Reform News Bulletin (2004), Carnegie Endowment Centre for International Peace, Washington, US, December, Vol 2, No 11.

Bayat, A (2000), *Social Movements, Activism, and Social Development in the Middle East*, Civil Society and Social Movements Programme, UN Research Institute for Social Development, November, Report No 3.

Bush, R (2004), *Civil society and the Uncivil State; Land Tenure Reform in Egypt and the Crisis of Rural Livelihoods,* Civil Society and Social Movements Programme, UN Research Institute for Social Development. May, Report No 9.

Choubaky, A (2004), *Future Scenarios for the Muslim Brotherhood, Following its Appointment of a New Leader,* Centre for Political and Strategic Studies, Cairo, Egypt, Report No 6, January 6–22.

Cook, S (2004), *The Unspoken Power: Civil-Military Relations and the Prospect for Reform,* Brooking Institute, Report, No 7, September.

Cunningham, A (2005), *Economic Reform in Egypt, 2004–2005,* paper presented at the annual BRISMES Conference, University of Durham, September.

Egypt's Succession, Part 1: Will Egypt follow Syria's Precedent, Middle East Media and Research Institute, Inquiry and analysis, July 24th, No 31, 2000.

Egypt's Succession, Part 2: Does Gamal Mubarak Have a Chance?, Middle East Media and Research Institute, Inquiry and Analysis, July 25th, 2000.

El Diwani, R (2003), *Islam in Egypt,* Internal Report, Chatham College, Pittsburgh, February.

Gutner, T (1999), *The Political Economy of Food Subsidy Reform in Egypt,* FCND, November, Report No 77.

Brown, N, Hamzawy, A and Ottaway, M (2006), *Islamist Movements and the Democratic Process in the Arab world: Exploring the Gray Zones,* Carnegie Endowment Centre for International Peace, Washington, US. March, Report No 67.

Hamzawy, A (2005), *The Key to Arab Reform: Moderate Islamists,* Carnegie Endowment Centre for International Peace and Democracy, Report, No 40, July.

Hamzawy, A and Brown, N (2005), *Can Egypt's Troubled Elections Produce a more, Democratic Future?,* Carnegie Endowment Centre for International Peace, Washington, US, December.

Hassan, M (2005), *Outlawed and Outspoken: the Muslim Brotherhood in Pursuit of Legal Existence and Intellectual Development in Egypt,* Middle Eastern Department, UC Berkeley, Report, December 15th.

Hawthorne, A (2004), *Is Civil Society the Answer?,* Carnegie Endowment Centre for International Peace, Report No. 44: pp.1–24.

Heydeman, S (2003), *Towards a New Social Contract in the Middle East and North Africa,* World Bank Report Unlocking the Employment Potential in the Middle East and North Africa. Report, September 19.

Human Development Reports: Arab States 2002, *http://hdr.undp.org/reports/detail_reports.cfm?view=600*

IMF, *Approves 24-month Stand-By Credit for Egypt,* No 96/50, October 11, 1996.

International Crisis Group (2003), *Challenge of Political Reform: Egypt after the Iraq War,* International Crisis Group, No 9, September, 30th.

International Crisis Group (2005), *Reforming Egypt; in Search of a Strategy,* International Crisis Group, Middle East and North Africa, No 46, 4 October.

Kamar, B and Bakardzhieva, D (2003), *Economic Trilemma and Exchange Rate Management in Egypt,* Annual conference of the Economic Research Forum for Arab Countries, Iran and Turkey, December 16th-18th, Marrakesh, Morocco.

Keller, J and Nabli, M.K, (2002), *The Macroeconomics of Labour Market Outcomes in the MENA Region over the 1990s,* 4th Mediterranean Development forum, Amman, Jordan, October, 6–9, *www.worldbank.org/wbi/mdf/mdf4./*

Kheir-El-Din, H (1996), *The Social Fund for Development: Assessment of Performance and Impac*t, Egypt-Human Development Report (Research Paper Serious). Egypt: Institute of National Planning and UNDP.

Kodmani, B (2005), *The Dangers of Political Exclusion: Egypt's Islamist Problem,* Carnegie Endowment Centre for International Peace, Washington, US, October, Report No 63.

Koh, H (2001), *Advancing Democracy: the Clinton Legacy,* Carnegie Endowment Centre for International Peace, Washington, US, January 21st.

Korayem, K (1997), *Egypt's Economic Reform and Structural Adjustment (ERSAP),* The Egyptian Centre for Economic Studies, October, No 19.

Licari, J (1997), *Economic Reform in a Changing Global Economy,* OECD, Development Centre Working Papers, December, Report No 129.

Ottaway, M (2003), *The Problem of US Credibility, Middle East Series Promoting Democracy in the Middle East',* Carnegie Endowment Centre for International Peace, Report, No 35, March.

Overseas Development Institute (1996), *Adjustment in Africa: Lessons from Ghana?* Report, 3rd July.

Oweiss, I (1990), *Egypt Economy: The Pressing Issues,* The Political Economy of Contemporary Egypt, Center for Contemporary Arab Studies, Georgetown University, Washington, D.C. (Online) *http://www.georgetown.edu/oweiss/epe/epe.htm*

Qandil, A (1996), *al Dur al Siyasy li Jama'at al Masaleh fi Misr: Dirasat Hala li Niqabat al Ateba, (*The Political Role of Interest Groups in Egypt: A Case Study of the Doctors Syndicate), Cairo: Al Ahram Center for Political and Strategic Studies 1996.

Social Fund for Development (1999), Annual Report 1998. Egypt.

Sowa Kwaku, N (2002), *Assessment of Poverty Reducing Policies and Programs in Ghana,* paper presented in a conference on assessment of poverty reduction policies organised by INSEA and IDRC under micro impacts of macroeconomic adjustment policies (MIMAP) project, Rabat, Morocco, January 28–31st.

Tamimi, A (1999), *Islam and Democracy, Jordan and the Muslim Brotherhood,* Kyoto University, Japan, July 17th.

'*The Grooming of Gamal Hosni Mubarak',* Middle East Media and Research Institute, Inquiry and Analysis, No 141, July 8th, 2003.

The National Intelligence Council of the CIA (2004), *Mapping the Global Future,* December.

USAID/Cairo/EAS, Report on *Economic Conditions in Egypt, 1991–1992* (Cairo: USAID, 1993), No. 2.

World Bank (1991), *Egypt: Alleviating Poverty during Structural Adjustment*, Washington, D.C: IBRD.

World Bank (1996), *Implementation Completion Report*, Egypt: Structural Adjustment Loan. Loan No. 3353-EGT.

World Bank (2000), *World Development Indicators*, Washington, DC: USA.

World Bank, (1995), *A.R.E.: Country Economic Memorandum: Egypt into the Next Century*, Report No. 14048-EGT, May 1995.

Theses (PhD and MA):

El Gafawari, I (1999), *Structural Adjustment in Egypt; The Case of Agriculture*, Doctorate Thesis, Department of Politics and International Studies, University of Leeds.

Majdalani, R (1999), *Bridging the Gap Between the Development Agendas and the Needs of the Grassroots: The Experience of Jordanian NGOs* (Beirut).

Michael, S (2002), *The Role of NGO's in Human Security*, Paper for the Commission on Human Security, Harvard University, Cambridge, MA, May.

Stacher, J (2001), *Moderate Political Islamism as a Possible New Social Movement: The Case of Egypt's Wasat (Center) Party* (MA: Cairo: American University in Cairo).

Magazines and Newspapers

'A Judicial Intifada', *Al Ahram Weekly*, 27 April-3 May, Issue No, 792, 2006.

'A Return to the Centre', *Al Ahram Weekly*, 9–15 December, Issue No, 459, 1999.

'After the Elections', *Al Ahram Weekly*, 15–21 December, Issue No, 773, 2005.

'A Revolution to End the Revolution', *The Economist*, October 25th, 1997.

Al Hayat, September 28th, 2000.

'Al Wefaq to field 19 candidates', *The Voice of Bahrain*, The Gulf Daily News, October 6th, 2006.

'All Politics is Local', *Egypt Today*, March, 2006

'Amnesty says Egypt 'Muzzling Society', *BBC News*, September 19th, 2000.

'Analysts: Egyptian Gov't to curb ME further Political Gains', *Al Mesryoon*, May 30th, Cairo, 2006.

'An Elusive Euccess', *Al Ahram Weekly* 29 December–4 January, Issue No, 775, 2006.

'Back with a Vengeance', *Al Ahram Weekly*, 10–16 March, Issue No, 733, 2005

'Band of Brothers', *The Guardian*, December 9th, 2005.

'The Bar Association take Two', *Al Ahram Weekly*, 24–30 March, Issue, No, 735, 2005.

'Bush Administration concerned with the issue of Mubarak Absence', *Al Dostor*, August 11th, 2006.

'Campaign Promises', *The Arabist*, August 26th, 2005, http://arabist.net/archives/2005/08/18/campaign-promises/

'Catching the Islamist Train', *Al Ahram Weekly*, 26 October–1 November, Issue No 244, 1995.

'Catchword Change', *Al Ahram Weekly*, 30 September–6 October, Issue No, 449, 1999.

'Change at Hand', *Al Ahram Weekly*, 23–29 September, Issue No, 709, 2004.

'Chronicle of a Result Foretold', *The Economist*, August 25th, 2005, http://www.electronic-economist.com/displayStory.cfm?story_id=4321913

'Clashes at Egypt Judicial Protest', *BBC News*, April 24th, 2006.

'Clashes Erupt as police attack demonstrators supporting Judges', *The Daily Star*, April 27th, 2006.

'Crisis of Leadership', *Al-Jazeera*, broadcasting on December 4th, 2002.

'Dealing with a New Reality', *Al Ahram Weekly*, 24–30 November, Issue No, 770, 2005.

'Debating the Future', *Al Ahram Weekly*, 15–21 May, Issue No, 638, 2003.

'Economic crisis loom over Egypt Campaign', *Iran Daily*, September 4th, 2005.

'Economic Reformers rise in Egypt', *BBC News*, July 14th, 2004.

'Egypt – The Rise of Gamal Mubarak's Technocrats', *allbusiness.com*, January 23rd, 2006.

'Egypt extends emergency law as crackdown on protestors continues', *Ikhwanweb*, May 2nd, 2006, http://www.ikhwanweb.com/Home.asp?zPage=Systems&System=PressR&Press=Show&Lang=E&ID=4420

'Egypt extends emergency law', *Al Jazeera*, April 30th, 2006.

'Egyptian PM suggests way to sideline Islamists', *Arab Online*, June 1st, Dubai, 2006.

'Egypt journalist jailed for libel', *BBC News*, February 23rd, 2006.

'Egypt: Investigate election fraud, not judges', *Ikhwanweb*, May 4th, 2006. http://www.ikhwanweb.com/Home.asp?zPage=Systems&System=PressR&Press=Show&Lang=E&ID=4430

'Egypt: State targets opposition amid calls to extend emergency law', *Reuters*, April 30th, 2006, www.alertnet.org

'Egypt's Cautious reshuffle', *BBC News*, July 14th, 2004.

'Egypt's crawl from autocracy', *Opendemocracy*, August 30th, 2005.

'Egypt's Judges in election protest', *BBC News*, April 20th, 2006.

'Egypt's ruling party pledges reform', *BBC News*, September 29th, 2003.

'Egyptian court sentences Ayman Nour to five years', *Daily Times*, December 25th, 2005.

'Egyptian presidential candidates launch campaigns', *Voice of America*, August 17th, 2005, www.voanews.com

'Egyptians begin asking: After Mubarak, what? Debate focuses on successor, Chances for democracy', *Washington Post*, December 17th, 2003.

'Engineers demand elections', *Al Ahram Weekly*, 3–19 April, Issue, No, 790, 2006.

'Establishment of the Muslim Brotherhood', *Ikhwanweb*, March 15th, 2006, http://www.ikhwanweb.com/Home.asp?zPage=Systems&System=PressR& Press=Show&Lang=E&ID=4091

Egypt's New Government to Pursue Economic Liberalisation not Political Reform, *Democracy Digest, Weekly News Bulletin*, July 23, No 12, 2004.

EXCERPTS, from the speech made by President Hosni Mubarak in Menoufiya on Thursday 28 July announcing his intention to nominate himself for a fifth term, *Al Ahram Weekly*, 4–10 August, Issue No, 754, 2005.

Fahd Fanek, 'Who wants democracy in the Arab world,' *Jordanian Times*, (Amman, Jordan), September 30th, 2002, FBIS Transcribed Text.

'Fighting for Civil Space', *Al Ahram Weekly*, 6–12 June, Issue No, 589, 2002.

'Gamal Mubarak takes credit for father's victory', September 30th, 2005, www. arabnews.com

'Gamal Mubarak', *Al Jazeera*, March 29th, 2005.

'A New Boost for Privatization', *Al Ahram Weekly*, 7–13 December, Issue No, 511 2000.

'Glimpses into the history of the Muslim Brotherhood', *Ikhwanweb*, March 1st, 2006, http://www.ikhwanweb.com/Home.asp?zPage=Systems&System=Pre ssR&Press=Show&Lang=E&ID=3989

'Going it alone', *Al Ahram Weekly*, 6–12 April, Issue No, 789, 2006.

'Hamas sweeps to election victory', *BBC News*, January 26th, 2006.

'Hassan al Banna', Ikhwanweb, March 31st, 2006, http://www.ikhwanweb. com/Home.asp?zPage=Systems&System=PressR&Press=Show&Lang= E&ID=4187

'Hassan al Banna: A lasting legacy' *Reflections issue*, March 4th, 2005, www. mabonline.net

'Hezbollah wins easy victory in the elections in Southern Lebanon', *Washington Post*, June 6th, 2005.

'Husayn Abd-al-Wahid, 'Democracy and US Interests!' *Akhbar al-Yawm*, (Cairo, Egypt), August 31st, 2002, FBIS Transcribed Text.

'In Search of the Civil', *Al Ahram Weekly*, 8–14 November, Issue No, 559, 2001.

'Inner circle in Syria hold power and perhaps peril', Washington Post, October 28th 2005.

'Interview with Condoleezza Rice by James Harding and Richard Wolfe', *Financial Times*, September 23rd, 2002.

'Islamic Movement in Egypt in the 21st Century', *Shia News*, April 22nd, 2001.

'Islamists Forecast Harsher Crackdown', *The Daily Star*, June 28th, 2006.

'Islamism in Transition', *Al Ahram Weekly*, 11–17 March, Issue No, 420, 1999.

'Jordan Islamists Stir Tensions by Displaying Election Skills,' New York. *Times*, May 12, 2006.

'Like Father, like son?, *Al Ahram Weekly*, 7 –13 October, Issue No, 450, 1999.

'Local Councils in limbo', *Al Ahram Weekly*, 16 –22 February, Issue No, 782, 2006.

'MB Conundrum', *Al Ahram Weekly*, 10 –16 November, Issue No, 768, 2005.

'Meeting the Press', *Al Ahram Weekly*, 5–11 August, Issue No, 702, 2004.

Monitors vow at open poll booths, *The Voice of Bahrain*, Gulf Daily News, November 17th, 2006.

'Mubarak looks West for election tactics', *The Telegraph*, London, September 4th, 2005.

'Mubarak's reform promises backslide', *Middle East Online*, April 20th, 2006.

'Mubarak's son attacks Brotherhood', *Al Jazeera*, January 25th, 2006.

'Muslim Brotherhood to 'fight' Mubarak's efforts to hand power to son', *Haaretz*, October 13th, 2005.

'Muslim Brotherhood: Egypt arrests members', *The Mercury News*, April 29th, 2006.

'Muslim Brotherhood; we are a power in Egypt', *Al Jazeera*, June 22nd, 2005.

'Muslim rulers asked to adopt democracy; US narrows choices', *Dawn*, November 12th, 2003.

'New Brotherhood Arrests', *The Arabist*, June 19th, 2006.

'NDP launches campaign', *Al Ahram Weekly*, 2–8 November, Issue No 245, 1995.

'Nasser and the Brotherhood', *Al Ahram Weekly*, 27 June-3 July, Issue No, 592, 2002.

'Nazif pumps up the volume', *Al Ahram Weekly*, 2–8 February, Issue No, 780, 2006.

'New tests for Egypt's opposition- embattled Nour puts hope in vote for parliament', *Washington Post*, September 24th, 2005.

'Nour Jailed for 5 years for forgery', *www.arabnews.com*, December 25th, 2005.

'One Way Street', *Al Ahram Weekly*, 7–13 July, Issue No, 750, 2005.

'Party's old guard prevails', *Al Ahram Weekly*, 20–26 October, Issue No, 765, 2005.

'Playing by the Rules', *Al Ahram Weekly*, 23–29 December, Issue, No, 461, 1999

'Political Business', *Al Ahram Weekly*, 7–13 June, Issue No 537, 2001.

'Political reform tops agenda', *Al Ahram Weekly*, 16–22 March, Issue No, 786, 2006.

Quoted in 'reform in the Arab and Muslim world; Arab press reacts to national security advisor Condoleezza Rice's statements on democracy and freedom, *The Middle East Media and Research Institute*, Washington, October 11th, No. 427, 2002 . http://www.memri.org/reform.html

Mideast Mirror, November 18th, 2002.

'Regulating or Restraining?', *Al Ahram Weekly*, 7–13 November, Issue No, 611, 2002.

Revolution and the Modern Islamic movement', *Daily Times*, August 1st, 2004.

'Rifaat El-Said: Which way will he bend next?, *Al Ahram Weekly*, 7 –13 July, Issue No, 750, 2005.

'Roundup: Mubarak's presidential campaign highlights economy', *English People's daily online*, August 24th, 2005, http://english.people.com.cn/200508/24/eng2005082 4_204259.html

'Sameh Ashour: The boundaries of respect', *Al Ahram*, 14–20 July, Issue No, 751, 2005.

'Self-doomed to failure', *The Economist*, July 6th, 2002.

'Shia alliance wins Iraq elections', *The Guardian*, January 20th, 2006.

'Smiles for the family, a fiery warning for the world', *The Guardian*, January 21st, 2005.

'Speaking in Tongues', *Al Ahram Weekly*, 6–12 November, Issue No, 663, 2003.

'Speaking to the future' *Al Ahram Weekly*, 29 September–5 October, Issue No, 762, 2005.

'Stage set for political dynasty in Egypt? Signs may indicate Gamal Mubarak being groomed to succeed father', *NBC News*, July 28th, 2004.

'Stomping on Democracy in Egypt', *Ikhwanweb*, May 12th, 2006, http://www.ikhwanweb.com/Home.asp?zPage=Systems&System=PressR&Press=Show&Lang=E&ID=4466

'Strange Bedfellows for the Bar', *Al Ahram Weekly*, 23–29th December, Issue, No, 461, 1999.

'Syndicate Syndromes', *Egypt Today*, Vol 27, Issue 06, June, 2006.

Talal, S, 'The American 'Advice' Turns the Closure into Assassination,' Al-Safir (Beirut, Lebanon), September 9th, 2002, FBIS Transcribed Text.

'The Cabinet's New look', *Al Ahram Weekly*, 15–21 July, Issue No, 699, 2004.

'The Muslim Brotherhood and Egyptian Society', *Ikhwanweb*, April 3rd, 2006, http://www.ikhwanweb.com/Home.asp?zPage=Systems&System=PressR&Press=Show&Lang=E&ID=4215

'The Rich and the Brotherhood', *Al Jazeera*, December 14th, 2005.

'Top Egypt Judges face poll rebuke', *BBC News*, April 18th, 2006.

'Trading on Promises', *Al Ahram Weekly*, 25–31 August, Issue No, 757, 2005.

'Vague Comfort', *Al Ahram Weekly*, 22–28 January, Issue No, 674, 2004.

'Violence mars round two', *Al Ahram Weekly*, 14–20 December, Issue No 251, 1995.

'Who's Afraid of the Brotherhood', *Al Ahram Weekly*, 24–30 November, Issue No, 770, 2005.

'Winds of change blow through Egypt politics', *BBC News*, May 20th, 2005

'Young Minds, Open Debate', *Al Ahram Weekly*, 8–14 May, Issue No, 637, 2003

Websites

www.weta.org/worldtalk/transcript062603.html, 26th, 2003.

IMF, Article IV Consultation with the Arab Republic of Egypt. Public Information Notice (PIN) No. 01/116. November 5, 2001. (Online) *http://www.imf.org/external/np/sec/pn/2001/pn01116.htm*

Kefayah: al-Haraka al-Masria min Agl al-Tahir *http://harakamasria.org/*

The World Guide, 2001/2002, CDROM

Speeches

Dick Cheney's, Speech at the *World Economic Forum* Annual Meeting, January 24, 2004.

President Bush's Speech on Freedom in Iraq, *National Endowment Centre for International Peace and Democracy*, November 6th, 2003.

President Bush's Speech on Iraq policy, *Royal Banquet House*, November 19th, 2003.

Transcript of Bush's Speech to the American Enterprise Institute, *New York Times*, February 27, 2003.

INDEX